FLOWERS
FOR
CELEBRATIONS

FLOWERS FOR CELEBRATIONS

DEREK BRIDGES

Photography by

TREVOR RICHARDS

EBURY PRESS · LONDON

Published by Ebury Press
Division of The National Magazine Company Ltd
Colquhoun House
27–37 Broadwick Street
London W1V 1FR

First impression 1988

ISBN   0 85223 688 3

Editor: Susan Fleming
Designer: Bill Mason
Illustrator: Haywood and Martin

Filmset by Advanced Filmsetters (Glasgow) Ltd
Printed and bound in Italy by New Interlitho S.p.a, Milan

CONTENTS

INTRODUCTION   6

THE BASICS OF FLOWER
ARRANGING   9

CREATING A WELCOME   16

WEDDING CHURCH FLOWERS   33

BRIDAL FLOWERS   68

FLOWERS FOR WEDDING
RECEPTIONS   89

FLOWERS FOR PARTIES   112

CHRISTMAS   142

PLANT GLOSSARY   155

INDEX   157

INTRODUCTION

'To celebrate', according to the dictionary, can be 'to observe with solemn rites' or 'to honour with ceremonies or festivities'. The word 'celebration', therefore, can be happily applied to many diverse occasions, ranging from the solemnizing of a marriage in church, chapel or synagogue, to a formal anniversary dinner party at home or a children's birthday tea in the garden. A celebration of any nature, involving as it does the bringing-together of friends, deserves an input of care, thought and love — and one major way of doing this, I believe, is to use flowers.

Flowers are fresh, alive, colourful and fragrant, their beauty a celebration of the glories of Mother Nature herself. Flowers extend a welcome in a uniquely joyous way, and I can think of nothing more celebratory and calculated to please than an arrangement of flowers. Flower arranging is my business, after all, so I could be said to be biased.

The celebrations for which I have arranged flowers in the following pages fall into two main groups: entertaining guests at home — for dinner or buffet parties, for Christmas and other selected anniversaries — and weddings, perhaps the occasions with which we most associate celebratory flowers. A party at home for friends can be a simple or more elaborate affair, but by using flowers, you are turning your home into a place of enjoyment and fun, your own enjoyment of the occasion reflecting in the vivid memories your guests will have of a wonderful welcome. Arranging the flowers for church, bridal party and reception is a lot more ambitious,

A homely yellow arrangement in a basket brightens up a landing. Into soaked
floral foam in a flat plastic bowl inside the basket, I placed western hemlock for
the outline foliage, along with some forced early broom. Yellow Dutch irises bring
the eye in towards the central placements of yellow carnations and my beloved
gerbera.

obviously, but not out of the question if you are enthusiastic enough! (But I don't advise this if all you have ever done before is arrange a table centre for Christmas!)

You are entertaining guests at a celebration because you wish to be with them and to give them pleasure; you are arranging flowers because you love working with fresh plant materials and wish to use their beauties to decorate and extend a welcome. Flower arrangements are, after all, an opportunity to show off what Mother Nature started – using the raw materials to display them at their glorious best. All it requires is patience, prior organization and an expression of your, perhaps occasionally hidden, talents.

I have suggested a few ideas in the following pages which I hope will entertain you, expand your own floral repertoire, and set your imagination working. Flower arranging is *not* an exact art, nor is it one of rigid rules: it is an art of imagination, of adaptation, of individual 'feel' and 'eye', with an infinite capacity for variation. I hope that not only will my ideas help you with your flower arranging in general, but will help, too, with better party-giving. Remember, though, flower arranging is not just what you know, it's what you've still got to learn. This applies to me too – I'm not an expert, I just know a little about what I'm doing – and *my* celebratory ideas are here to inspire *you*.

Derek Bridges

THE BASICS OF FLOWER ARRANGING

Most of you will know the basic 'rules' of the art – and the captioned photographs in this book will enlighten you further about the principles involved in individual arrangements – so I'll concentrate briefly on the necessities. The most important of these is the conditioning of the plant materials themselves, treating them so that they will last *once arranged. Other considerations are how to buy the best materials; the mechanics or aids to make your arrangement keep and hold its shape; and the containers in which you will make your arrangements.*

BUYING PLANT MATERIALS

When buying from the flower shop, a few words of advice will not go amiss. I always give a wide berth to flowers that are displayed in their boxes outside the shop: poor things, lying there, possibly in the hot sun, what chance have they got? I'm also not keen on flowers being kept in cold storage, those freezer-type cabinets that you see in some flower shops: how long have they been there, I ask myself.

If you're buying spring flowers, look out for a certain transparency: this means they are getting a little old. If you look at the back of the flowers and they are showing some green colouring, they will be fine to buy. Try to buy bulbous spring flowers in bud – it's such a joy to watch the flowers open. Daisy-shaped flowers – a great favourite of mine, as you'll discover, reading through the book – should have hard stamens tinged with green, which shows the flowers are young: if the pollen is powdery, they are 'going over'. Fortunately, growers have at last recognized the correct picking time, and the time flowers take to get to the markets, and many flowers are now being picked in the young state so that they will last well. Roses and anemones, however, are the exception and should not be picked when young: they should be bought when the flowers are showing colour.

CONDITIONING PLANT MATERIALS

The ability of all flowers and foliages to last well in arrangements – whether bought from the florist's shop or plucked from your garden – depends entirely on their conditioning. All plant materials need *at least* twelve hours in water before being arranged (I sometimes leave flowers in for days). Take a bucket with you into the garden (in morning or early evening preferably) holding about 12.5 cm (5 inches) of cold water, and put flowers and foliage in immediately they are cut. Fill the bucket up with cold water when you get back to the house, and leave in a cool place for the requisite time.

Most flowers, either florists' or garden, will take up water well if you just re-cut the stems with a slanting cut. This exposes a larger drinking surface. Woody stems can be slit with a sharp knife, but I don't like bashing the ends of stems as some recommend – I 'feel' for the flowers. Bulbous flowers, mostly spring flowers, are usually bought with some white stem from near the bulb: this should be cut off to enable them to take up water better.

Stems which exude sap need to be sealed. Hold the cut ends over a candle flame or gas flame. Plunge into cold water.

There are some flowers that need very special treatment. These are those with stems that bleed when cut, the main family being the euphorbias, of which there are many varieties. Sealing the ends of the stems is the answer, and there are two ways in which this can be done. Either stand the cut stems in boiling water for a few seconds, or burn the stem end with a candle flame or gas flame. Plunge immediately into cold water. (Do this with poppies as well, and they will last much longer.) I am also often asked about the hellebores, again a big family. Firstly, do not pick them too young. To ensure that they last, prick with a pin just behind the head and at various intervals down the stem, and then plunge them into deep cold water up to their necks. The same thing can be done with tulips, a pin prick behind the head, but don't put them into such deep water. The last two that I shall single out are the violet and the hydrangea. They like their heads wetting: spray them with a syringe or gently dip the heads into cold water, shaking off the surplus before putting the stems into deep cold water.

Many blossoms will last much longer if their foliage is removed, and lilac, weigela and philadelphus come straight to

Prepare flowers and foliage by stripping off all surplus foliage with a sharp knife. Cut stem end with a slanting cut.

mind. If you want the leafless stems to feel at home, though, pick sprays of just foliage, so that you will have flowers on one stem and leaves only on another. With many of these woody stems I like to give them the boiling water treatment which, by the way, is also very useful for flowers that are beginning to look wilted.

The last little idea to pass on is one used by Ikebana arrangers, and that is to cut the stems under water – I mean the stems under water, not you! This, I understand, successfully prevents air locks in the stems.

Now, having taken the trouble to prepare your flowers and foliages well – and don't forget, I have only suggested a few basics – you must continue to take care of them once they are arranged. For, however long they have been conditioned and however well, once they are arranged they will drink up the available water very quickly indeed. Do look at the arrangement every day and top up when required. Spray them occasionally too, with a fine mist, just as you do your houseplants.

AIDS AND EQUIPMENT

With interest in flower arranging increasing year by year, there is a greater range of equipment – or mechanics – available to aid flower arrangers. In many cases it is now very easy to arrange flowers, so I do urge you to start a good collection of some of the more common pieces of equipment.

The first thing is a good pair of scissors, with a good pair of secateurs and wire cutters. (Some people use their scissors to cut wires, but I don't, the scissors can be ruined.)

Floral foam comes in many shapes and sizes.

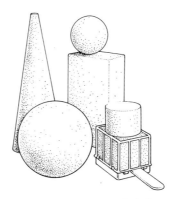

Wire netting is inexpensive, and is so useful for very large arrangements, either used on its own or as a 'hairnet' over floral foam.

Floral foam, probably the best thing ever for the flower arranger, is a must. It is a water-retaining medium sold under several brand names. It comes in various block sizes, and as balls and cones, and it can be cut to particular required sizes. Floral foam must be thoroughly soaked before use, though: I think it should be immersed in cold water for at least 20 minutes, or until the bubbles cease rising. It can be used as many times as it will hold together in one piece, but do remember that it must be kept moist between arrangements, in a plastic bag. If it is allowed to dry out, it will not take up water again.

Styrofoam, or a dry foam, is available as floral foam, but must *not* be soaked. It is used for dried flower arrangements.

Pinholders come in many sizes and shapes and are now mainly used by the Ikebana arrangers or for the modern 'line' arrangements in flat dishes. Always remember that if you are fixing a pinholder into the container with plasticine, the container, pinholder and plasticine must all be perfectly dry.

Floral foam tape – which is adhesive – is used for anchoring floral foam or wire netting into a container. Florist's stem tape is, as it sounds, the ideal material for covering wire stems. It is *not* adhesive.

You should have florist's wires in various gauges and lengths, and also on the reel. You will see through the book where I have found all types of wires useful, and they should be part of your first 'tool box', whether metal or plastic.

Cones or tubes, available in floral accessories departments, are very useful in large arrangements to create height. In the wedding section particularly, you will see how effective they can be.

Candle-cup holders are 'extra' containers, designed to go into a candlestick to make it into a flower container. A finial shape on the underside of the cup fits into most candlesticks, but might need the aid of some plasticine to create a wedge.

Garden canes, glue, pieces of wood, screws, etc, all, perhaps surprisingly, find a place in my battery of necessary equipment. You will see throughout the book how useful they have been!

A small watering can with a long spout is ideal for topping up the arrangements with water without damaging the plant materials. And a syringe or sprayer is also very handy. When the weather is warm, it will be a great aid to keep the arrangement fresh.

Lastly, a dust sheet. Whether you are arranging flowers at home or away, do be tidy – it looks good and it saves time.

CONTAINERS

It seems to be a natural course of events that when you take up flower arranging, you also take up looking for the unusual in which you can make a flower arrangement. Not only is whatever you find as a container to be part of the finished whole, but it must be capable of holding the arrangement together. I have been arranging flowers for some years, so my collection of containers is vast – and please notice that I use the word 'container', not 'vase'.

Containers fall into various categories. There are those

with stems, which range from the wine glass for a small arrangement in a bedroom, say, to something that could take a 3 m (10 ft) arrangement. I refer a lot in the book to bowl shapes with flat bottoms which are, I think, one of the most useful, not only by themselves, but also inside other containers – baskets and alabaster urns, for instance, both of which need a 'liner'. Bowl shapes are also useful for table arrangements where a higher container would not be suitable. Flat dish shapes are also handy for modern 'line' arrangements.

Many containers will be made of metal – silver, pewter and copper – all of them wonderful foils for flowers, the metal seeming to help the flowers last longer. Glass, the most popular medium some years ago, seems to have lost favour but can be used very well with carefully planned mechanics. Wickerwork and basketry containers (as some of you will know) are my favourites, and for natural informal arrangements, there is nothing better.

Essentially, my basic principle is that anything – yes, I *do* mean anything – that holds water can hold flowers. This can even be 'stretched' to encompass a piece of beautiful driftwood, to which a tiny container can be fixed. If you haven't already got that special flower arranger's collector's eye – seeing the containing and decorative possibilities of virtually *anything* – try to develop it: it's so much fun, quite apart from all else. In the following pages, you'll see how far I stray from the conventional vase!

CREATING A WELCOME

Entertaining at home is one of the major joys of every householder, and it's particularly suited to the flower arranger. For what are flower arrangers if not show-offs, and having guests — whether for a simple supper or drinks party, for a more formal dinner, or to stay for the weekend, say — is the ideal opportunity to display their talents and expertise!

ARRANGEMENTS FOR EVERY ROOM

Any occasion when you are surrounded by friends is an occasion for celebration and what better to capture that spirit than by decorating your home with flowers. I don't think that there is a single room in the house that *cannot* be decorated. Some of you perhaps associate only the main rooms with that special treatment — but not so. I do sometimes get very strange reactions when visitors go into the bathroom, though; little sniggers go around, as if to say 'even flowers in the bathroom' — but why not? It's the same in the kitchen, but again why not? I have always said that I'm taxed for the whole house, so I *decorate* the whole house!

Firstly, though, every home is different, as indeed is every flower arranger, and you must always complement decor, mood, and the *type* of occasion or celebration with your flowers. You can create an atmosphere with flowers, or at least contribute greatly to one, so design your arrangements very thoughtfully and carefully. My ideas, outlined in both words and pictures, may not suit *your* home, but I hope the basic concepts will enlighten you, stir your own imagination, and galvanize you into decorative floral action and adaptation!

The arrangements in the following pages are for creating a welcome – in the porch or hall, in bedrooms and, yes, in the bathroom. For more elaborate ideas, and for dinner and buffet parties, see pages 112–141.

THE PORCH

The welcome for your guests should start as soon as possible, perhaps with a welcome ring on the front door – see page 123 for one idea. Or you could utilize a very simple concept such as that on page 18 if you have a porch through which guests will pass into the house proper. A glass porch is a useful adjunct for the flower arranger who does not possess a greenhouse, as it is here that he or she can grow all those plants useful for foliage – the ivies and ferns from which to borrow the odd leaf or spray for a flower arrangement. I much prefer a *grouping* of plants to having individual pots dotted about all over the place – and I am fortunate in having a collection of white pottery urns which make good plant containers when not holding cut flower arrangements. When combined, the fresh greens of the white massed plants, along with the white paintwork and white urns in the picture, give a crisp, fresh welcome in spring or early summer.

THE HALL

Once through the porch, you're in the hall in most cases. If your hall is small, you may not feel it's big enough for people,

Above: Start your welcome to your guests as soon as you can. This grouping in a porch – of nephrolepis ferns, ivies and the prayer plant – gives a crisp welcome, the fresh greens against the black and white tiled floor. An idea to think about – and it's so simple!

Right: If your hall is big enough, have a bold welcoming arrangement, and the use of light here – the arrangement container is a lamp similar to the lit one – in unison with the warm autumnal colours of the flowers, creates a cheerful, warming atmosphere. The height was achieved with preserved beech foliage, and the bronze strap-shaped leaves of New Zealand flax. Sweeping out to the side are sprays of variegated ivy, and bronze bergenia leaves give weight to the centre. As this was a special occasion, I added sprays of green cymbidium orchids with brown noses which sweep up at the top of the arrangement. Carnations and bronze spray chrysanthemums lead in from the sides to orange gerberas and lilies ('Enchantment') at the centre.

let alone flowers, but do try to have something, even if it's only two roses in a stem vase – flowers create such a warm welcome. (You might like, too, to utilize some of the ideas in other chapters. There are photographs of hanging arrangements on pages 55 and 146 which could be adapted for use in a small hall.)

For the hall picture on page 19 I used a pair of spelter figurine lamps, which are amongst my favourite containers. Yes, lamps *can* be used as containers; it's an easy job to unscrew the lamp fitting and replace it with a large candle-cup holder. (These come in metal or plastic and are shaped like a scoop with a protruding piece at the end which fits into the hole where the candle is. Put a ring of plasticine round the protruding piece first – this acts as a 'glue' to keep the holder in place – then cut a piece of floral foam to fit the scoop, anchoring it across the top with floral foam tape.)

As both figurines were tall and weighty looking, I could afford to create a large bold arrangement, with strong spine lines for height, and larger flowers. Note how interest is created by having the lamps at different levels, the one holding the arrangement on the floor, the other on a small table set against the wall. On a cool autumn evening, with the lamp light falling on the warm autumn colours of the flowers, what a welcome this would give.

THE STAIRCASE

Many halls contain the stairwell and staircase, and for a special occasion you could make this a feature, alongside a complementary arrangement if you like. In the autumnal

To wire a leaf, pierce either side of the main stem at the back with a 'stitch' of wire. Bring the legs together in a hair pin shape.

To wire a flower, pierce the calyx with wire and bend two legs together in a hairpin shape.

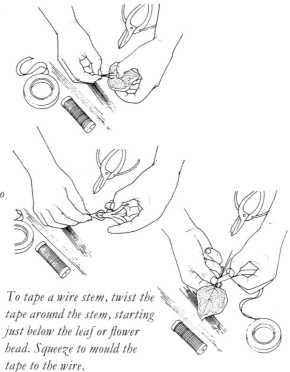

To tape a wire stem, twist the tape around the stem, starting just below the leaf or flower head. Squeeze to mould the tape to the wire.

welcome on page 23, the staircase leading from a sitting room, in fact, I have used dried, preserved and silk materials to make both a staircase garland and a matching pyramid arrangement, both complementing the room colourings.

You will see garlands often throughout the book – in church for weddings, at the wedding reception, and at Christmas – and once you have mastered the way in which they are made, you can adapt them to many usages. On pages 49–52 I describe how to make fresh garlands and how to prettify *bought* artificial garland lengths; here I tell you how to construct a dried garland. Swag, perhaps, would be a more exact description, as it is stronger and more solid, to lie straight rather than sweep as would a garland.

The first necessity for items to be included in a swag or garland like this is a leg or stem. Many dried items already have their own stems, and silk leaves and flowers too come with stems. With individual dried leaves, seed pods or pine cones, however, you will have to *make* a stem, and this is done with florist's wire – reel or stub, depending on the weight of the individual item. To wire a leaf, fresh or dried, take a piece of silver florist's wire. In the back of the leaf, about one-third

A hall with a staircase – here a sitting room with a staircase – can be decorated with a welcoming swag or garland, along with a matching arrangement if you like. The swag, made of dried and preserved materials and silk flowers bound on to garden cane, was made to the length of the banister and fixed into position with ribbon loop ties so that the woodwork was not damaged. The complementary pyramid, in a spelter urn, uses the same materials, and both garland and pyramid together make a magnificent welcome group that can be re-used again and again!

of the way up, carefully pierce either side of the main stem with the wire, and bring the two legs together to where the main stem is. On the front side of the leaf, you will be able to see a small 'stitch', and on the back of the leaf a hairpin shape. Keep one wire straight alongside the natural stem (if any), and twist the second wire around the natural stem and the first wire. Twist in a clockwise manner as if winding up an old gramophone. Straighten the wires out and you have a supported leaf with a wired stem. A pine cone is given a leg by forcing a length of florist's stub wire between the row of scales nearest the stem end. Take it half-way round the cone and then bring the wire ends down and together at the foot of the cone, and twist round a couple of times to make a leg. To give seed pods legs, pierce a soft pod through the pod itself, near to the stem; wind wire round the stem of a hard pod as for a pine cone. To give fresh or dried flowers a stem, see one idea on the previous page.

To disguise the wire and its metallic sheen, cover the stems with florist's stem tape (in green or brown). Lay the end of the tape over the wire just behind the item. Twist the stem to catch the loose end, and then squeeze so that the heat of your hands moulds the tape to the wire (it's not actually adhesive). Spin the wired leg, stretching the tape and spiralling it around the wire, until about two-thirds of the stem is covered. Break off the tape.

Once you have collected a huge profusion of wired and taped items – for you'd be surprised how *much* material is needed for swags and garlands – you can start to bind on to the chosen garland base. Many such decorative effects can be made simply by taping the ingredients on to wire but here,

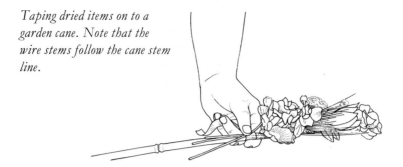

Taping dried items on to a garden cane. Note that the wire stems follow the cane stem line.

because the desired effect was bigger and bolder, because the ingredients were heavier, and because the ultimate length was to be about 2.4 m (8 ft) – to cover the relevant piece of stair handrail – I built the group on to a straight garden cane.

Lay the cane (or wire) on your work surface with all your prepared items close by. Pick up the individual leaves or seed pods one at a time, lay the wired stem against the cane, and bind the two together with florist's reel wire as in the drawing. When you have wired on a couple of items, you can then cover the wires and cane with florist's stem tape. (With lighter, wire-based garlands, you can simply bind spine wire and wire stems together with tape, two steps in one.) Continue along the cane (or wire), varying the materials, and keeping an eye on its balance and shape, until the garland is complete. Do use as great a variety of plant materials as possible, as this is where the interest lies. Here, in both garland and pyramid, I used about 60 different items (thus rather space-consuming to list entirely), which included pine cones, dried poppy heads, Cape gooseberries, dried artichoke bottoms, ferns, and wheat ears along with silk flowers to lighten the symphony of natural creams and browns. Fix the swag to the stair handrail, leaving the stair side free, with ribbon straps, here made of hessian, so that the wood is not damaged.

The pyramid shape of the complementary arrangement is one I am very fond of, and it's so easy. You can buy cone shapes already cut out of styrofoam, or you can cut your own to the size desired from large blocks of styrofoam. Here I used four blocks, which I carved to shape, and then encased in wire netting – to hold the blocks together and to give a

This large pyramid has various pieces of carved styrofoam as a base. These can be held together by 3 thin garden canes pushed through the middle, or by garden wire netting, as here.

more secure base for the materials. These were fixed on to a container on top of a spelter metal urn with climbing cherubs – one of a large, much loved collection. When these mechanics are firm and stable, start the arrangement by doing about three circles or layers of the plant material near the container rim, then choose and place the right slender materials from the spine top. In most pyramid shapes you would want to have larger materials near the base, graduating to smaller as the cone diminished in size towards the top; here the materials are roughly the same size throughout. Your next placement should be about three layers or circles down from the top. After this, you have a bottom and a top, and all you need to do is fill in, to bring the two areas together, with the remaining plant materials. Always make sure you have plenty of material – pyramids '*eat*' them – and do take care to keep the shape very regular. This arrangement is now a permanent fixture in this sitting room, needing only an occasional pat with a feather duster – and the garland is kept fresh in a tissue-lined box, coming out for high days and holidays!

THE LANDING

If you haven't decorated the staircase, the landing – half-way up the stairs, or at the top – is a possibility for a floral decoration, especially if you have friends staying for the weekend. If it's a darkish corner, flowers will brighten it up; if it's got a window – as in the homely yellow basket arrangement on page 7 – your welcome will be all the more cheerfully apparent. Just think about how many times you go up and down the stairs during the day, and you will appreciate how effective an arrangement could be in this position.

As in any basket arrangement – even those in church (see page 43) – the arrangement should be informal and fairly casual, with gentle flowing lines. In this yellow welcome for spring, I used one of my favourite flowers – gerbera – and I am always being asked how I condition them. I have outlined this in my other books, but it is worth repeating, as I think they respond so well. Use the tallest bucket you can find, three-quarters fill it with water, and cover the top with a piece of wire mesh. Re-cut the gerbera stems and stand the stems in boiling water for 10 seconds. Immediately drop them through the wire mesh so that the heads rest on the wire and the stems dangle down into the water. After twenty-four hours the gerberas will be in super condition – I have had some respond to this conditioning by lasting for over a month!

The Bedroom

You may demur at the thought of flower arrangements in bedrooms, but I think they look lovely all the time, let alone when you are entertaining. Years ago it wasn't the done thing to have flowers in the bedroom as they were supposed to take all the oxygen – but I always have flowers around when I'm sleeping, and I'm still here! A little arrangement in a room for guests staying the night will show how much you care – and even an arrangement in the bedroom designated for coats and/or nose powdering will impress and beautify. Don't ever be too elaborate, though, that would be out of keeping with

A pink bedroom colouring and a lace table cover are echoed in a simple, pink,
'country' arrangement. Some fern sprays were 'borrowed' from plants in the porch,
and used as outline foliage. The flowers were daisies, pinks and Peruvian lilies with
the delicate white bobbles of Bristol fairy. I tucked a couple of lacy bows in, a
linkage with the lace in the room.

When making ribbon bow loops, keep the ribbon pinched between forefinger and thumb as you make the loops with your other hand.

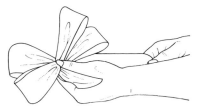

most bedrooms, even those with huge four-posters.

In a simple feminine – and youthful – room, an arrangement with similar qualities is called for, and in the photograph on page 27, you can see how the lace in the room and the pink colourings are echoed by the 'laciness' and pink of the arrangement. It has a country feel about it, and looks as though I've just been out in the garden and gathered what I could find.

I don't often use ribbon bows *in* arrangements as here, but I do use them a lot in other contexts, so it's worth describing here how to make them. The principle is the same for *all* ribbon bows, whatever finished size they are, or whatever width ribbon you are using.

Gather together your container or reel of ribbon, and some florist's stub wire. To make a 10 cm (4 inch) bow, pinch the ribbon between forefinger and thumb of one hand 10 cm (4 inches) from the end. (If making a larger or smaller bow, pinch at the required length from the end of the ribbon.) Make a loop the same length with the other hand and pinch between the same thumb and forefinger. Keep going with the ribbon across the forefinger and thumb, pinching the same length of ribbon each time you cross the centre, until it looks like an aircraft propeller! Make three loops on either side of the finger and thumb, six in all, and cut off surplus ribbon, leaving another 10 cm (4 inch) length as tail. (These tails, of course, if you want them to trail as streamers, could be very much longer.)

Still holding all the ribbon loops in the fingers, take a piece of the wire and put it across where you have been holding the ribbon. Push the wire downwards on both sides, trapping the ribbon in the rounded head of a long hairpin shape. Push the petals upwards and twist the wire stems down and together, creating the stem and trapping the loops in the wire. Put a finger into each loop and pull into shape. Use the wire stem to place the bow into the floral foam as you would a flower stem, or to attach the bow on to a garland etc.

In a second bedroom arrangement overleaf, you can see a prime example of 'togetherness', a concept which you will encounter many times in this book. Colourful flowers decorate the wall, and I have tried to emulate these in the basket flower arrangement. What a nice cheerful welcome for any guest staying with you, and even nicer if you give them the arrangement to take home. If this is your intention, do remember to leave the handle free and clear – it's visually attractive anyway, but makes the arrangement so much easier to carry.

Incidentally, while we're talking about bedrooms, there are many who live in bed-sitting rooms, the classic bedsits, in which they both socialize, eat and sleep, and there's absolutely no reason why these shouldn't have celebratory flower arrangements as well. Perhaps, as there's so much going on in one small area, the arrangement needs to be scaled down in proportion.

THE BATHROOM

Another room that is neglected when it comes to flower arranging is the bathroom. If, again, you're dubious about decorating the smallest room in the house, all I can say is why not! Many bathrooms are a bit spartan or antiseptic, but I

*Above: A basket arrangement looks so at home in this Victorian country
bedroom, and the colours of the fresh flowers echo those in the wall covering. A
large margarine container was secured into the basket, and held the floral foam. A
long-lasting leather fern was used for the outline and for recession. The flowers –
chosen for their lasting properties, as the arrangement makes a good parting
present for your guests – are carnations, pinks and spray chrysanthemums.*

*Right: An interesting bathroom arrangement – which complements the shapes and
colours of the wall covering, and the collection of Maltese glass. Echoing the
movement of the whirls of colour in the glass are the whirling shapes of dried bean
pods, fitted with wire stems. This leaves as much room as possible in the glass tops
for the thick stems of the pincushion proteas. I love these flowers, but sadly they
cannot be dried as can so many of their family.*

think they can and should be made to look good, just as any other room in the house. It's a room your guests will visit — perhaps more often than a bedroom, say! — so let your creative talents loose here too.

In the photograph on page 31 I have echoed the flowers of the wall covering and its colours in an interesting arrangement of fresh and dried materials. This in turn echoes the colours and whorls of the brown glass, a collection made in Malta. There was enough interest already created in the bathroom by the wall covering and the varied glass objects, but the addition of the natural plant material, rather than swamping the glass, *increased* the visual interest. The only foreseeable hazard is that, by making the bathroom too beautiful and comfortable, guests will be inclined to linger longer, and a queue will form!

WEDDING CHURCH FLOWERS

According to some, weddings are out, old hat, passé. Not in my opinion, though! I suppose I am rather biased for, having this great love of flowers, I think weddings and flowers go together so inevitably and naturally. In fact, ever since I became interested in flowers (long before I took up actual flower arranging), I have loved a good wedding, revelling always in what the flowers looked like, rather than the guests!

Planning in Advance

It is one of the highlights of my week to trundle off to cathedral, church, chapel or synagogue to do the flowers for a wedding – and it must also be one of the greatest challenges and joys for any flower arranger. It's such a happy occasion, after all, and there is usually a profusion of wonderful materials to work with. As you may have gathered, I love flower arranging for weddings – and by now I'm rather experienced! – but nevertheless I still believe firmly in planning very well in advance. All sorts of things have to be considered and taken into account: the wedding budget, the wedding colour scheme, the style of church, the requirements, needs and tastes of both bridal party *and* vicar, priest or rabbi.

The budget must come first. If it is limited, then I would think in terms of one or two large arrangements; if you have a freer hand, then you can have great fun planning all sorts of floral decorations over all the available areas. The colour scheme of the wedding is vital too, as the 'togetherness' I always try to achieve is nowhere more relevant than at a wedding, with bridal party colour themes to be echoed by bouquets, flowers in church, flowers at the wedding reception, the colour of the marquee lining (if that's relevant) etc. The style of church to be used for the wedding is an important consideration as well, for if it is large – a cathedral even – bigger and more striking flowers or arrangements will be necessary, and the lines of a modern building, for instance, will need to be echoed by your designs. You must also check with the vicar, priest or rabbi where he will *allow* arrangements to be put, and even the numbers on the guest list is important to you, the flower arranger, as this again will determine to a certain extent the placement and size of some arrangements.

So, as you see, it is no easy task, and you can appreciate why I quite often like to have up to three months in which to plan everything very precisely. (After all, my reputation is at stake!) Speak to the bride, learn what she wants and what she can afford; visit the vicar and then the church, looking it over for likely areas etc, and for the finished effect you would like, then you can begin your designing.

The first thing to remember is that in a large area such as a church, the arrangements must be *seen*, so big is beautiful. Small flowers and small arrangements will just disappear. People will be at a distance from your arrangements, rather than feet away as at home, so design them with this very firmly in mind. This long-distance viewpoint, however, does not

A view down the aisle towards the altar, showing the alternating pew-end arrangements, the twin pedestals on either side of the chancel, the breathtaking arrangement on top of the chancel screen, and a hint of the glories at the altar. From this, even though quite near the front of the pews, you will appreciate what I mean when I say that church flowers and arrangements need to be larger and bolder — simply in order to be seen!

35

mean that you can get away with using half-dead flowers, or not covering up the mechanics: you have to complete the arrangements properly, but you don't have to go into *quite* as much detail as you would in those that are viewed at close quarters. Remember too that the church will be full of people on the big day itself, so you want your arrangements to constantly be in view and appreciated. Although floor based arrangements *can* be stunning, some will quite disappear when the congregation is standing and singing. In the following pages, I describe and illustrate many different types of church flower arrangements for weddings, all of which should give you ideas and set your own imagination working!

Once the wheels are in motion, and all the details have been worked out on paper, the planning still doesn't stop. Indeed, in the weeks just prior to the wedding, you will have to work your hardest. Check whether there will be a wedding before or after yours that day (usually a Saturday): if there is, try to liaise with all the other parties, to keep everything friendly. If the church has a flower rota, find out whose turn it is and let them know it's their weekend off – they should be thrilled! Find out where the water is, and the brush and shovel – very important because, if you leave a mess, they won't be happy to see you back on some future occasion. You will have ordered the flowers already; do be sure, though, to give the florist one or two alternatives if what you have chosen is unusual or out of season. You don't want to panic when the flowers are delivered two varieties short!

The preparation days of the final week before the wedding are the most labour intensive. You should get all your required containers together, cleaned and ready to take the wire mesh or soaked floral foam. It is a good idea – if it's possible – to take all these and your other equipment along to the church the day before arranging day, say, and get the containers into position – the more that can be done beforehand the better. Your foliage – such an important part of any flower arrangement – will be conditioning (see page 10): I think nothing of sometimes having foliage in water conditioning for as long as five or six days in advance of it being arranged. In fact, if you have limited space at home, see if it's possible to have a 'dumping ground' at the church; it will save a lot of trailing around with wet foliage on the day. The same could be said of the flowers when they are picked up from the flower shop: if the powers that be are agreeable, take them straight from the shop to the church and condition them there. This saves so much hassle on the arranging day itself.

Try to make this arranging day the day *before* the wedding. So much could happen if you left it until the last minute, and if you are even a few minutes off your schedule, you might panic, cut corners, and not be happy with your finished work. With a whole day in front of you, you can relax and work at your own speed. Put your groundsheet down at the position of your first arrangement, and gather together all you need. Don't rush, and do take a break when you have done so much that nothing will go right, or if you're tired. I always take a snack with me, and the paper, so that I can have a proper relaxing break – and there is always a refreshment area at the big flower festivals for that very reason. After a rest you can return to the next session with renewed vigour and lots of enthusiasm.

Flowers for the Country Church

The country church I decorated for a wedding is St Mary's, Luddenden, West Yorkshire. The colour scheme I chose in consultation with the bride was green and white, and if you feel this part of the wedding section is a little more generous in space and pictures than others, then I have to admit that the bride happened to be my daughter, Sara!

It is a fairly small church, traditional in architecture and internal fittings, and thus the arrangements had to be designed to suit. The flowers used were chrysanthemums and carnations, lilies (*longiflorum*), gladioli, irises, Bristol fairy (*gypsophila*), marguerites, and a delightful new arching michaelmas daisy *(aster)* called mini-mic, now being grown on a commercial basis. All were in white – it was a Yorkshire wedding after all! The foliage used was ivy *(hedera)*, ferns, hosta, box *(buxus)*, spider plant *(chlorophytum elatum)*, beech *(fagus)*, and lady's mantle *(alchemilla mollis)*, the latter used both for its foliage and its branching heads of star-shaped flowers. Throughout the church I used different combinations of the same flowers and foliages in different arrangement shapes and sizes to suit individual settings. I hope many of these will give you lots of ideas which, obviously, you can happily adapt to your own situation and colour schemes.

Chancel and Screen

Let us start with this area, the most used during a wedding, for this is where it all happens apart from the couple's private moments at the altar. This area will be the focus of all eyes

*Simple, triangle-shaped arrangements for the altar, one on either side of the cross, will look most effective from a distance. In a white bowl, into soaked floral foam, I created the height with gladioli, the width with white carnations and filled the centre with lilies (*longiflorum*). To reduce the flower weight, I introduced a little Bristol fairy with, trailing out to the sides, lengths of ivy. Western hemlock and hosta are additional foliages.*

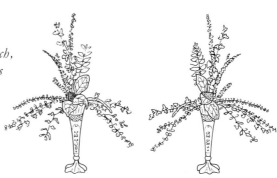

Always work on a pair of arrangements in tandem so that you achieve a good match, with symmetry, proportions and balance correct. Here foliage creates height and width, and note how the features are reversed.

during the main part of the ceremony, acting as a frame for the bridal couple, and so this is always where I would spend most money. I also think there is nothing to beat the lovely traditional, big and bold pedestal arrangement, one on each side. In fact, if a limited budget demanded only *one* area or arrangement, this is the position I would choose – all my eggs in one basket, so to speak!

The twin arrangements on either side (see page 35) must be worked in tandem, *vital* to get them to look the same. They are big, bold and striking, and you can appreciate why I emphasize large flowers, especially in the centre – smaller ones would just disappear. The pedestals too – ideal for churches – stand about 2.4 m (8 ft) high, and can still be seen when the congregation is standing. The outline foliage is beech, one of the best you can use for large arrangements in my opinion. It should never be used too young, however. You *can* pick sprays when it is in bud and force it into leaf, but once past this stage, it is best to leave on the tree and pick and use when the foliage is mature – from about late July onwards, I would say.

Once the outline foliage had been placed, large hosta leaves were put in the centre both for visual weight and to help cover the mechanics of the arrangement. These, by the way, must be *strong* in any large flower arrangement. You don't want the thing to topple over! When you are satisfied with the shape, the same lines must be followed with the flowers, starting at the top with something pointed, in this case gladioli, which are also used at the sides to give width. I gradually worked in towards the centre with spray chrysanthemums and spray carnations until I came to the focal part of all massed arrangements, the centre. Chrysanthemums, lilies and carnations were interspersed with Bristol fairy and lady's mantle. Remember that it is the variety of shapes and sizes that makes these massed flower arrangements so super to do and which creates such a stupendous visual effect.

As you can see in the same picture, I also decorated the very beautiful screen top. This idea would not work in all churches, but if given permission to use this area, it looks wonderful – and in this case was, I think, the hit of the wedding! I had placed long plastic troughs containing blocks of soaked floral foam on the top of the screen, and topped them up with water before the arrangement was started. Here again you have to go for effect, for no-one is going to climb a ladder to have a close look – although with some types, you can never be sure... The lovely Bristol fairy and lady's mantle were used in great profusion with arching sprays of mini-mic. It looked beautiful!

THE ALTAR

This is the next most important area, I think, after the chancel and screen. It must be treated with respect, and consultation with vicar or priest will determine where the flowers can be placed. Many churches no longer like to have flowers on the altar itself, but prefer them displayed to the sides – on tables, say, or pedestal stands. Here I did both, with twin arrangements on either side of the cross (again, as with the chancel pedestals, worked together), and various arrangements massed to both sides of the altar table.

The area around the altar table or to the sides can be used to great effect. Here I have massed four arrangements – all in the wedding colour scheme and with the chosen flowers – at different levels, one on the floor even, despite my hectoring on this subject!

*A window-sill arrangement in a basket, with an inscription behind which acts as a
baffle to the light, which can cause problems for arrangements in areas such as
these. The outline is formed by large graceful green ferns, gathered from the local
woods, and the beautiful lime-green of lady's mantle sweeps to the side. Weight in
the centre is added by large hosta leaves, green apples add interest to the sides and
green grapes to the front. The flowers are white irises and spray carnations.*

43

*Fill an altar vase or narrow-
necked tall vase with water,
then cut a piece of floral foam
into a cone shape. Soak it, then
wedge the point in the vase, the
wide end upwards to take the
arrangement.*

Although the altar is important, it is a very long way away
from the congregation, so you are wanting to create an effect
only. The altar arrangement itself (see page 39) is a simple
triangular shape, held into a low bowl with soaked floral foam.
Incidentally, if you have to use those brass altar vases – which
many flower arrangers find very difficult – I've come up with
the ideal solution. As most of them are tapered, cut the piece
of floral foam into a long cone shape, soak it and then wedge
it into the brass vase, point downwards. With water already in
the vase, the cone shape will stay permanently wet. My other
piece of advice is to use thin-stemmed flowers only because, if
you're not careful, the floral foam could fall apart.

In the picture on page 42, you can see how I've used the
space *around* the altar to great advantage. The arrangements
are beautiful up close, and shimmer attractively in unison
from a distance. The floor area itself, of black and white tiles,
is a very good foil for arrangements of any colouring.
Although I am a great believer in getting church flowers up
high, there are occasions when lower arrangements have their
place – as here! The various arrangements at the different
levels give great interest and create a whole design, but each
can be seen individually to advantage. The arrangement
around the candlestick is interesting, I think, because it flows
away from the candle, giving a nice gentle line, but also
allows the candle to be lit and to burn well.

WINDOW SILLS

The sills in a church are probably a nightmare for most flower
arrangers. After many years, however, I've become quite

fond of them! There are a number of problems to be overcome, not least the light coming through the window into the back of the arrangement – which can usually kill the arrangement completely. Sometimes, in fact, it is best to leave such sills well alone, and spend the money elsewhere. But you can often make a backing for the arrangement from a piece of hardboard, cut to follow its sweeping lines, and stained a natural colour. This cuts out the light at the back of the arrangement, without plunging the church into total darkness. On one of my country church sill arrangements, though (see page 43), there was an inscription at the back of the window sill which solved the problem for me, giving a good backing, and ensuring that nothing from the arrangement was lost.

I used baskets for the containers – unusual perhaps for a wedding, but why not? – and I echoed this theme with brides-maids' baskets (see page 71). One advantage of using baskets is that they can be anchored on so well, for another of the major horrors of church sill flower arranging is that most such sills are sloping. In the picture on page 47 of the all-green sill arrangement you can see how potentially difficult this could be, but in fact here I was lucky as there were small condensation drainage holes in the stone. Into the centre one I wedged a small wooden peg with a length of strong wire attached to it, and fixed the wire on to the back of the basket to hold it in place. A container was then fixed into the basket: this had to be deep sided because it would be at a slight angle, and I didn't want a flood while the wedding was going on!

I like the idea of all-green arrangements in the slightly rustic baskets – appropriate in this instance in the country

Above: A pew-end arrangement in the green and white colour scheme of my country wedding. Once the outline shape had been achieved, I put in the ribbon bows, in green with green and white streamers. The flowers are spray carnations and pompon chrysanthemums, Bristol fairy, mini-mic and lady's mantle. The foliages are mixed ivies and a commercial, market-bought leather fern.

Right: A window basket arrangement, fitted on to that bane of the flower arranger's life, a sloping sill. Here, although using the same outline foliages of fern and lady's mantle with hosta leaves in the centre, polished green apples were used just like flowers as a focal point. I really liked this all-green effect, which could be used at any time of the year — think about it for harvest festival, for instance.

church, but a nice idea for any time of the year. Fruit was featured here – see page 149 for more details about how to mount fruit and vegetables for flower arranging – and I also used ferns, wild ones gathered from a local wood. I am often asked about the use of ferns in flower arrangements, particularly about when to pick them. I think they should only be picked when they are mature, when the brown spores on the backs of the fronds are dusty and pollen-like. As with many plants picked from the wild, they need a good conditioning – at least two days in water – before being arranged.

PEW ENDS

I used to hate pew ends so much that I would do everything in my power to dissuade brides and their mothers from having them. Large nails were out, so we had to make do with tape and glue and prayers that the arrangements would stay in place. Now, however, all that has changed, and the whole thing is very easy both for me and for you. There are plastic containers on the market, oblong plastic boxes with handles. They were originally designed as funeral spray holders but flower arrangers, being an ingenious lot, soon adapted them to pew-end use. Some of the boxes have floral foam already in them, some you will have to tape foam in. In either case, the foam should be soaked first, and thereafter I usually let them hang for a while to drain off excess water – saves enormous pools of water up the aisle! Treat pew-end containers as any others for flower arrangements, making them on the table, and then hanging them – don't kneel on the floor, that's too much like hard work. I also find it best to do all the pew-end groups together: the outline foliage in them all first, then the outline flowers and so on. Don't complete one and then go on to another, they never turn out so well.

In the picture on page 35 you can appreciate what effect the alternating flower pew-end arrangements and ribbon bows will have on guests coming into the church – and what a greeting for the bride! Once again, as in the close-up picture on page 46, I have used the theme flowers of the wedding – spray carnations and pompon chrysanthemums, mini-mic, Bristol fairy and lady's mantle. All the ribbon bows can have been made in advance, and boxed ready for use (see page 28 for detailed instructions on how to make).

GARLANDS

Garlands have been a form of floral decoration for centuries, and they make a wonderful wall decoration in many circumstances and at many times of the year – think of them at Christmas! They are particularly effective when used to decorate the canopy in synagogues for Jewish weddings (some of the happiest and best I have done flowers for over all my flower-arranging years). In my country church, I utilized garlands in quite a few areas, to great effect I thought.

There are various ways in which garlands can be built up. You can, for instance, obtain long lengths of plastic tubing into which you thread pieces of soaked floral foam, tying the tube off after each piece so that you end up with a long string of sausages. Foliage and flowers can be pushed in through the plastic and, at the end of many hours' work, you have a fresh

Above: A close-up of the fresh material decorating the artificial garland: sprays of variegated ivies create flowing lines to the side, bunches of shiny glass grapes and green apples provide central interest, with the added drama of a 'sunburst' of spider plant leaves.

Left: A spectacular idea for wall or pillar decorations in church – a simple garland with an artificial foliage base, decorated at intervals with fresh material and topped with huge green and white ribbon bows. The only problem concerns those who might be frightened of heights!

garland. Another method makes use of washing line. This is very easy, but you can only use foliage that will stand well out of water – pine and cypress, for instance – with fresh flowers pushed in at the last moment. Measure the length of line that you need to complete the garland, and fix one end of it to a door knob or around a nail hammered into the workshop bench. Have at the ready a large amount of conditioned foliage as above, cut into 15–17.5 cm (6–7 inch) lengths. Take up one piece of foliage and bind it on to the line with florist's reel wire, then follow with another. You carry on thus, walking backwards, as the line is covered and the garland is created. When it is secured in place, and only then, you can attach flowers or fruit etc, whatever takes your fancy. Flowers can just be pushed into the green foliage, but fruit will have to be wound on with wire. Do make sure, when using heavy fruit, that it is absolutely secure; you don't want anyone to be knocked out in the middle of the service by an apple proving the laws of gravity, the wedding might be transformed into a funeral!

The most spectacular use of the garlands in this context was as a pillar decoration running from the decorated ceiling of the church to the floor. It is very simple and its base is artificial foliage, which can be bought in long lengths. Dark green in colour, it can be used at any time of the year. At intervals along this base I attached sprays of various ivies, groups of apples and grapes, and spider plant leaves. You can see the detail on page 51, and the overall effect on page 50. It's simple and dramatic.

Other uses of these same artificial garlands can be seen on page 55, in the entrance arrangement, and on page 54, at the back of the church. As you must constantly remind yourself, no two churches are ever the same, so that there is no one guideline I can give when organizing the flowers. *My main guideline, however, is always to make the most of what I have.* Here, at the back of this particular church, there was a wonderful stone wall which, in my opinion, was just crying out to be used for something. As it's at the back, you may well ask who will see it? Don't forget that the bridal party have to leave the church, and how nice it would be to have something for them to look at as they process down the aisle.

I made two three-tiered wooden stands which I thought would give rather an interesting effect. Each stand had a straight wooden back on to which three different sized wooden shelves were screwed, and then bracketed to the wall; these then took lightweight plastic dishes and the floral foam. The three separate arrangements of graded sizes in the photograph were made up of the more delicate plant materials of the wedding theme, along with marguerites, and a background of small ferns and box foliage. The garlands were used between the two arrangements, forming a good link and preventing a too spaced-out look. (This tree effect idea could of course, be used at any time of year: see what I've done with the same shape for Christmas on page 147, or you could make it with a lovely collection of mixed Christmas foliages, some berries, red carnations and a red ribbon bow – very festive.)

THE CHURCH ENTRANCE

Flowers for celebrations should always be welcoming and, although I've left it to virtually last, there is no reason why

*A pretty tree-like effect formed from three arrangements of graded sizes on a
wooden tiered stand fixed to the wall. The plant materials used are more delicate –
lady's mantle, Bristol fairy, spray carnations and marguerites – and the foliage is
small ferns and box. (See page 148 for instructions.)
The garland links one 'tree' with another, creating a coherent design.*

In an entrance hall with limited space – whether church or home – you could get
round the problem by having a hanging arrangement, perhaps in a basket as here.
In a container of soaked floral foam are placed the more delicate and light plant
materials – ferns, variegated ivies, lady's mantle, Bristol fairy, mini-mic,
marguerites and carnations. The whole effect is united by the use, once again, of
garlands, ribbon bows and streamers. Note that the dark colouring of the garland
is lightened by the addition of some dried sea statice.

you shouldn't have some welcoming flowers at the entrance to the church. In some churches, of course, there is no entrance hall to speak of, and indeed here, it was rather narrow, with steps climbing on either side of the main doorway to the gallery and the bell tower.

A floor arrangement wasn't considered, therefore, but an eye-catching something that wouldn't be an obstruction was possible – and what better than a hanging basket? In the picture on page 55 you can see how I suspended the basket from the wrought-iron balustrading. I then worked the arrangement from all around the basket as it would be seen from both below and above. I used the more delicate plant materials as I wanted a light effect, and the artificial garlands again – this time made to look a little different by intertwining them with dried sea statice. Green and white ribbon bows complete the picture.

If, however, there is space in an entrance, you might like to consider a pyramid arrangement such as the one on page 58. The garden urn base is in fact plastic, but I sloshed it with various odd paints, sand and soot – a messy job (but fun) – and it looks very realistic. The pyramid isn't really tricky to achieve, just rather fiddly, and a matter of getting the mechanics correct and stable. The whole arrangement is about 1.8 m (6 ft) tall, and the height is achieved by various mechanics – bamboo garden canes and plastic flower cones of about 25 cm (10 inches) long. Firstly, to save having to fill the urn with floral foam (such a waste), I managed to find a plastic bowl to fit the top. This was filled with soaked floral foam, then wire mesh was placed over this to give a good firm base – the arrangement *is* rather heavy and powerful. On to the bamboo canes I attached five flower cones with floral foam tape, at different levels, and into these cones I made my arrangements, which together form the pyramid shape, grading upwards with flowers and foliage from the main body of the arrangement. As with all arrangements, but particularly in something like this, you have to use flowers of the right size: to achieve the effect and shape I wanted here, I introduced large bloom chrysanthemums as a feature flower. Each cone is filled with water but the only trouble with a large arrangement such as this (I *have* done one of 6 m/20 ft in height) is that you have to remember how many cones you have used in order to top them up with water to keep the arrangement alive.

OTHER WEDDING FLOWERS

Thus far, I have covered in detail the green and white wedding – which I hope will have given a strong idea of a consistent colour scheme and all that it entails. It must certainly have clarified the amount of forward planning needed, even for one occasion in a small country church (although that occasion *was* rather special for this particular flower arranger).

Not all weddings, of course, need so much work, and you can choose only one from the ideas illustrated and discussed. All churches are different – I can't emphasize this enough – and it may be that budget, space or just sheer aesthetics dictate one large arrangement. In the cathedral setting on page 59, as with all church flowers, big is beautiful – but what I particularly like here is the *space* around the arrangement: the

By using bamboo canes and plastic floral cones, you can build up an arrangement into this striking pyramid shape. The trickiest part is keeping the shape as you work your individual arrangements in the separate cones. Here, in five cones, are arranged gladioli and bells of Ireland for the height, with carnations and bloom chrysanthemums as the main flowers. Bristol fairy adds that sparkle, and the foliage weight is laurel.

In a larger church such as a cathedral, arrangements have to be bigger and bolder to achieve the right effect. Here, atop a wrought-iron pedestal stand, height is achieved by gladioli to give the upright lines, with sprays of ivy sweeping down to the sides along with the graceful lines of ruscus foliage. Spray carnations and spray chrysanthemums complete the outline with, towards the centre – to achieve the massed, solid-colour effect – gerberas, carnations and dahlias.

size of the building and of the designated area made this possible, but it allows the arrangement to make a much more positive statement, and to be seen properly!

The large pedestal stand has been used as the basis for an autumnal wedding arrangement – wonderful strong and deep colours for a flower arranger after the softer shades of summer. Height is the most important thing here, and to cope with this the mechanics must be very sound: take time when preparing to ensure these foundations and then you will have a happy – and stable – arrangement. To achieve height, you might want to consider using the bamboo canes and plastic cones described above – and do remember to top up the cones with water before leaving the church. Here, however, I used a sturdy large container filled with soaked floral foam and covered with wire mesh. Gladioli were used for height, to carry the eyes up, and sprays of ivy and a lovely foliage, ruscus (grown under glass), sweep to the sides. In arrangements of this size, you need to have a bold and solid centre, so look for flower size or flower quantity. I wanted a massed effect, so quantity and solid colour won the day.

In any church, other features can be singled out for decoration with flowers – the font or the pulpit, say. Both are usually striking – whether modern or traditional – although every font and every pulpit is quite different in shape and size, and no definitive guidelines can be given. I'm sure, for instance, that a whole book could be written on the subject of pulpits: I've seen and arranged flowers round many beauties over the years, made of stone, wood, metal – even a glass one, would you believe!

The pulpit on page 62, as you can see, is a modern one which

I thought needed rather special treatment. The wood colour had to be complemented – just as a stone or metal colour would too – and I decided to complement the colour of the purple cloth as well, with deep summer pinks (that togetherness again, I can hear you saying). Rather than overpower the structure with one large arrangement, I chose to do two, the larger on the floor of the pulpit, the smaller one on the top. Both, of course, had to be as unobtrusive as possible so that they wouldn't get in the vicar's way – and the top one especially had to be extra secure so that it didn't go flying if the vicar gesticulated enthusiastically during his sermon. I strapped the container on to the ledge with floral foam tape before the arrangement was started. I worked both arrangements together which, although these two weren't a matching pair, always works better: you can echo sweeps and lines and achieve a more harmonic effect.

Fonts, too, seem ready-made for the flower arranger, and come in all sizes. Do remember, though, to ask the church for permission first – many don't approve. Fonts can be decorated for a wedding if in a place where they will be seen – why they are included in this section – but don't forget, of course, that they could be similarly treated for a christening or for a flower festival. If you do have the opportunity to use one, try to think of something other than an arrangement in the sunken top, or around the rim. These can look good, but would be rather inappropriate for a christening: the vicar or priest will have enough to do controlling a wriggling bundle without the additional worry of your arrangement having an extra drink.

The font in the picture on page 63 illustrates another

On a modern pulpit, two flower arrangements complement the colours of the cloth and carved wood. Although not identical, both arrangements were worked together, one in a container fixed to the top ledge, the other in a container fixed to the floor of the pulpit. A gentle line was created to both outer sides of the arrangements by flowing western hemlock and heath foliages, and the spray carnations placed in sideways. Those lead into lovely deep pink gerberas and Singapore orchids in the centre, with spray chrysanthemums and purple carnations.

An unusual possibility for a traditional stone font — two arrangements at different levels. The top one has heath and prunus blossoms to the top and flowing out to the right, with spray carnations, roses and tulips as the main flowers. A little recessing was done with separate flowers of spray chrysanthemums, and a delicate outline was created with some Bristol fairy. A trailing pink ribbon bow is echoed by ribbons and bows, from which is suspended the second arrangement, in a plastic pew-end container, using the same flowers and foliage.

63

possibility – one arrangement to the side of the rim, and a second hanging down the front. These would look spectacular at a wedding, and wouldn't hamper the vicar too much at a christening. I used a low flat-bottomed container on the rim, secured with some blu-tack – just to be on the safe side. Although I don't normally use much ribbon in my work, I thought it succeeded here – and how delightful it could be at a little girl's christening, with all those pale summer pinks. The ribbon bow was placed first in the centre of the soaked floral foam, and then the arrangement was worked around it. The second arrangement was built into the plastic box used for pew ends, with echoing flowers and ribbons, all suspended from a good-sized ribbon bow.

In a smaller church or chapel, it will be better again to concentrate the floral decorations in one place. The double window sill arrangements on page 66 are a good example of this: complemented perhaps by a facing duo, a smaller area would be lightened and cheered by the fresh spring yellows. (If you wanted only one arrangement, though, remember to have the tall spine line following the line of the central stone mullion, and then flow the arrangement to both sides.) Here, because the sill was flat and the glass plain, I could create nice gentle flowing lines from both sides. Thus I chose good flowing and arching sprays of ruscus and western hemlock, and fixed them in floral foam in large flat containers – large because the sun would quickly evaporate the water in a smaller container. I used a variety of spring flowers, and I have also, perhaps unusually, included cut hyacinths (one of my pet aversions being three hyacinths stuck up in a bowl like three sore fingers). As the flowers develop, hyacinths get very top heavy, and so the fleshy stems need support if used in an arrangement. All I do is push a thin garden cane up the centre of the stem which does no harm to the flower itself, and still enables it to take up water. I think this is much better than using florist's stub wire on the outside of the flower stem, as it is often visible.

Finally, as I firmly believe *no* wedding is complete without flowers, I wanted to give you an idea for a possible registry office wedding. It may be that when the wedding is booked, flowers will already be included in the 'price' – but there's no harm in asking, and something unique and personal could be very special to the happy couple. I have done flowers for registry offices on more than one occasion, so it *can* be done. As the couple stand in front of a table facing the registrar, a low flat arrangement is best, in a low flat container – the couple and the registrar want to be able to see each other! The same idea could of course be utilized for the altar table in any other smaller wedding area such as a chapel – but never forget to ask permission first. See overleaf for one idea for a chapel or registry office.

To make a feature of a smaller church or chapel window, two matching arrangements can be very effective. Sprays of ruscus and western hemlock flow to the foot and towards the middle of the window, and broom also creates the height. Broom and Bristol fairy keep the outline delicate, and long-stemmed carnations, orange tulips, double daffodils and hyacinths complete the centre. I like these two arrangements very much – they look comfortable!

For the altar table in a chapel — or in a registry office, perhaps — this simple and low-flowing group in sunny spring yellows would be ideal. Spray carnations and creamy yellow irises flow gently to the sides, and pale yellow broom helps to keep the whole thing delicate. Double daffodils and freesia give weight to the centre with some small pieces of single spray chrysanthemums. (I don't mind using flowers like daffodils out of season, but I only use the single varieties.)

BRIDAL
FLOWERS

When you were discussing the flowers for the whole wedding with the bridal party, you will have also covered the subject of the flowers to be carried or worn by the bride and her attendants. In fact, if you're going in for the togetherness I'm constantly so enthusiastic about – a total coordination of colour and feel – what the bride and her bridesmaids are actually going to wear should be your starting point.

CHOOSING A COLOUR SCHEME

It's usually the bridesmaids who wear a colour, and this normally dictates the colour scheme of the flowers for the whole wedding. The fabric and shape of the dresses can suggest types of flowers, or the style of a bouquet, for instance – and the *look* of the bride-to-be herself can also be a guideline for the flower arranger.

The first interview with the bride is very important. This is when the initial ideas will be mooted, and you can begin to clarify what she has in mind. She may fancy a Victorian wedding dress, a Twenties one or even a mini – and whichever she plumps for, will give you your basic ideas. She may be influenced by fashion, which comes and goes all the time, or by topicality – there was a spate of Sarah Ferguson dresses, veils, bouquets and headdresses in the months following that famous wedding – and you might have to step in with a few more practical suggestions as to what will suit or not suit her. All the time you are with her, hopefully at a very early stage in the wedding plans, you can be eyeing her up, noting her height, hairstyle, her colouring, general style – and then you can give her your considered opinions as to what you think might be better or best. All brides are individual, they all want different things, and they will also want help, for they'll not have done this before! In the end, though, you've got to remember that it's *her* day, not yours!

BOUQUETS

The first thing of note concerning bouquets is the number of traditions, nay superstitions, involved with them. Lilies, for instance, make beautiful bridal flowers, but many brides – or, more importantly perhaps, their mothers – cringe at the thought. It's probably the connotations of tears and funerals, perhaps a little influenced by the fact that some lilies tend to smell rather unpleasant! Ivy, too, although it is one of the best and most interestingly variegated and supple foliages, is thought to be an unfortunate choice. And lilac, which would be delightful at spring weddings, both flower and foliage, is shunned by some, as is the wonderfully scented may blossom. This, a hawthorn blossom, is considered to be the flower of lovers (although some associate it more with sex), and also to signify the oncoming of spring, the death of winter, rebirth. What could be more appropriate to a bride? But the crown of thorns was thought to be made of may or hawthorn, so that might explain its unpopularity. Cow parsley or anthriscus, too, is considered an unlucky choice, but this may be more to do with its similarity to hemlock, which is poisonous. For a green and white wedding for which the budget was fast running out, I once did an arrangement in the font of may

A fresh flower bouquet for a green and white summer wedding, designed to balance the width of skirt and sleeves of the shimmering, floating, delicate silk organdie dress. Singapore orchids start off the tail with pearl sprays (to link with the pearls on the dress) and leaves made from stiffened georgette. Star-shaped stephanotis and 'Tiara' roses give weight towards the centre of the bouquet. Sprays of ivy, lily of the valley and Bristol fairy give a light and delicate outline to these bolder shapes.

*A bridesmaid's basket, painted white, with a handle encircled by tiny silk and
linen flowers, and a large net and ribbon bow. The arrangement itself, made into
soaked floral foam in the polythene-lined basket, is of fresh plant materials –
sprays of ivy, Bristol fairy and periwinkle as foliage, white roses, spray carnations
and freesias the flowers. Don't ever use too many flowers in baskets to be carried.
They, like the bride's bouquet, should never look or feel heavy to handle.*

blossom and cow parsley. It looked terrific, but I didn't dare mention a word to the bride's mother! (I still see the couple involved in that wedding, and they look all right to me.)

Bouquets themselves come in all shapes, sizes and types, and they should always, obviously, be designed in consultation with the bride, with her dress and her shape very firmly in mind. One of the most important things you will have to put across to her is that there will be a lot of frock, which the bouquet has to balance visually – so explain this to her when she asks for just a few flowers, 'I don't want anything big'. In the fresh flower bouquet on page 70 (for that Bridges green and white wedding, of course), I had to consider hard the question of balance because there was so much fabric in the skirt and in the magnificent sleeves. The fabric too – a shimmering and floating silk organdie – was another important factor, so the flowers had to be small and delicate. Large solid flowers would have been quite wrong. The bodice, panels at the hem and the sleeves were encrusted with flowers and pearls, so again this had to be thought about when designing the bouquet. It looked very beautiful – as did the bride.

For the bridesmaids at this green and white wedding I chose to arrange baskets, not long ago thought to be old-fashioned. (I don't care about that, it's what suits the girls and what the bride wants.) I painted the baskets white, more in keeping with the colour scheme than the natural colour, and decorated the handles with tiny silk and linen flowers. These were laid on the handle one at a time and bound on with very narrow ribbon. The nice thing about making a good job of baskets such as these is that after the wedding the bridesmaids

For a bridesmaid's basket, lay the silk and linen flowers one at a time on the handle, and bind on with thin matching ribbon between each. Do this before the fresh flowers are arranged in the basket proper.

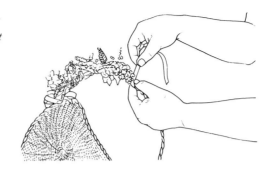

The completed tail of a bouquet with its empty taped spine to the top.

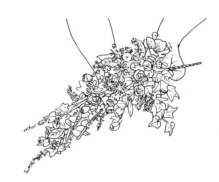

will have a pretty memento. A large net and ribbon bow suspended from the front of the basket (see page 71), and fresh flowers were arranged in the middle.

Many plant materials for bouquets, depending on the types, of course, need to be wired. In fact, at one time it was unheard of *not* to use wire, and I can remember in my early days spending hours wiring and taping boxes of individual flowers and leaves in readiness for the make-up work to begin. I can also remember using moss balls into which flowers and foliage were pushed – the only way, we thought, of keeping the bouquet together. Although bouquet making is quite advanced, it's not too dissimilar to making a swag. Just in case you want to have a go, I describe below – and in the drawings – the very basics of the process.

The first priority, as with all flower arrangements, is the conditioning of the plant materials to be used – they have to last well throughout all the bouquet make-up and throughout the entire wedding. The next thing to do is to wire the flowers and foliages. Use thin silver florist's wire, twisting it carefully around stems and flowers. To wire leaves, see page 21. Once

*A bouquet for a Christmas bride or bridesmaid, the colours and textures of which
would sing out on a dull and cold – or snowy – winter's day. The outlines are made
up with holly and ivy (naturally!), with long sprays of leafless red holly berries
and the traditional Christmas roses,* helleborus niger. *The swathe of plaid
ribbon through the centre echoes the ribbon streamers of the bridesmaid's
headdresses.*

A warmly coloured bouquet for an autumn bride — imagine this echoed by bridesmaids, warmly clad in russet velvet dresses! The ivy and Singapore orchids sweep naturally to the sides, and the centre is filled in with lilies ('Enchantment'), freesias, spray chrysanthemums, and cotoneaster berry clusters and leaves. The whole thing looks warm, interesting and colourful — quite a change from the bouquets consisting only of roses, lily of the valley and stephanotis.

The virtually complete top of the bouquet, the spine receiving its final taping.

The empty taped spines of both tail and top are bent down at right angles and the central flowers are added. The spine wires are taped together at the back, and the bouquet is complete.

all have been wired, cover the stems with florist's stem tape as described on page 22.

Once all this preparation has been done, keep the flowers in plastic bags until you start the assembly of the bouquet. For a wired bouquet, you need long pieces of a strong gauge wire for the spine. To this – exactly as for a swag or garland (see page 24) – the wired flowers will be bound. The top and tail are made first, the latter slightly longer than the former. Start with a pointed flower or piece of foliage and lie it against the piece of spine wire for the tail. Tape together with florist's stem tape, then lie the next flower in alongside, followed by the next and so on. Gradually work up the spine wire, all the time making the work slightly wider. By the time you have built up about 25–30 cm (10–12 inches), the tail is ready to put down (in the plastic bag) while you make up the smaller piece for the top. This piece will be about 12.5–17.5 cm (5–7 inches) long.

On both top and tail wires, you should have about a third of the wire left, with no flowers attached. Bend both of these spine wires down at right angles, bind them together, and this then forms the beginnings of the handle. At this stage, therefore, you have two groups of flowers with a gap in the middle, which is where you will build up the heart of the bouquet. As in a flower arrangement, this central or focal point is very important, so it is where the best and main flowers should be fixed and arranged. All their wire legs come together at the back at the handle area. When you are happy with the bouquet, tidy up the back, at the top of the handle, and bind the handle with ribbon so that the girl has something nice to hold.

Although wired bouquets are convenient in that the individual ingredients can be 'made' to do what you want them to, a more natural look is just as acceptable these days, with the flow of the fresh plant materials itself creating the bouquet's outline shape. In the photograph on page 75, you can see the very natural use of the ivy trails for instance, giving a graceful line and an easy movement. The same can be said of the Singapore orchids left in their natural sprays. The other interesting thing about this bouquet is its strong autumnal colouring – which could look fantastic with the right setting. For white or pale flowers aren't compulsory these days, as many brides seem to think. Others actually hate the thought of white flowers, thinking they will look 'dead' against the white of the dress – but in fact, white flowers against a sheer white fabric appear *cream*, as you can see in the picture on page 70.

I'm rather keen on strong colours for fabric for bridesmaid's dresses, particularly in colder weather or at Christmas – an increasingly popular time for weddings nowadays. I've often been asked to do Christmas wedding and I dread hearing the colours chosen (if I haven't been there

*A posy bouquet for a bridesmaid in deep colours, made up of mixed fresh and
artificial plant materials – anemones, cornflowers, heather, lilies, ivy, asparagus
fern and rose leaves. The headdresses, for bride and bridesmaid, echo the colourings
of the bouquet. The bride's coronet is made up of roses and spray carnations, with a
delicate filigree of dried Bristol fairy to lighten its outline. The bridesmaid's half
band contains roses and heather, all fresh, with a touch of blue artificial blossom –
to link it with the posy – and a blue ribbon to stream down the back of her hair.*

A natural looking and pretty, cream and peach posy for a bride. Made up of a combination of fresh and dried materials, fresh roses and freesias are the main flowers, with dried Bristol fairy, a selection of dried seed pods and fresh berry clusters adding colour and movement. The half band headdress echoes the colours and flowers, with the addition of a few rose leaves and a peach ribbon bow with streamers.

to express my opinions early enough): often I've had to cope with lemon or ice blue bridesmaids in the Christmas week – and I can tell you that the dresses often weren't the only things that were blue! I have also had some wonderful colours to work with, though, and at Christmas, what could be more interesting than dark green or maroon for bridesmaids' dresses – with which the bouquet on page 74 would blend perfectly. Set against the white of the bride's dress, with a bevy of bridesmaids carrying similar scaled-down bouquets and wearing matching headdresses (see page 86), any gloomy winter day would be cheered up enormously.

In complete contrast to the flowing natural style of the three bouquets described and illustrated so far, a posy shape could be considered. This would be more appropriate if it were to be a quiet wedding, with the bride perhaps wearing a short dress – and would be perfect if the style of a more traditional wedding dress were Victorian. Posies were very popular in Victorian times – with posy holders, posy vases etc – but they tended to be very tight with a central rose, orange blossom and sweet-smelling herbs bound together. The flowers had no room to breathe – mind you, that was how they managed their waistlines too!

Posy shapes have become very acceptable for both bride and bridesmaid, but I think they should be much looser and lighter, allowing air to flow through, and should look as natural as possible. The nearest I got to a Victorian posy is the blue and pink one in the photograph on page 78, designed to go with a fairly deep blue dress. This type of bouquet, as you might appreciate, is much easier to make up than a flowing one, as all the stalks (or wires) come down to a central point, and can be bound together to form a handle.

The cream and peach posy on page 79 is much more open and light, and looks almost as if I had gone out and gathered the flowers on the way to the church. The thing that I like about this posy is the combination of fresh and dried materials, which create a great deal of interest. Freeze-dried materials are now available to us – the Bristol fairy here is freeze-dried – and they keep much of their original colour.

One of the most important things to remember when making bouquets is that the bride and bridesmaids will have to carry their flowers for quite a long time, so they have to be as light as possible and balance well in the hand. Years ago, a finished bouquet was only considered good and right if it could balance across the top of the forefinger – I wonder how many of today's bouquets could achieve that perfection! The whole point, though, is that neither bride nor bridesmaid should have any trouble carrying their flowers – and certainly shouldn't have to hang on as if their lives depended on it! And, finally, the bouquet must *last* if it's fresh: the flowers should have been conditioned very well, and bound together very carefully. The bouquet is clutched in nervous hands, is put down, picked up again, so it must hold up to this treatment – and it mustn't look wilted in the wedding photographs!

HEADDRESSES

These too have become the province of the florist or flower arranger, most brides today wanting a togetherness of bouquet and headdress – and quite right too. Headdresses can

*The headdress worn by my daughter Sara is made entirely of artificial materials —
ivy, roses, lily of the valley, stephanotis, silk and georgette leaves, and sprays of
pearls to link up with those in her bouquet and with the decorations on her dress.
True togetherness!*

A bridesmaid's coronet which is a simpler and slimmer version of the bride's coronet opposite. Back interest is created by flowing streamers of lace ribbon which echo the ribbon bow on the basket she carries.

be either real or artificial, and by artificial I don't mean those things you can buy in millinery or bridal departments. I mean the headdresses which can be made up by the florist or flower arranger, using all their creative talents and those wonderful silk and polyester materials from the Far East. There's absolutely no shame attached to using artificial flowers – and when used properly they can be stunning. Just look at the bride in the picture on page 82 – and I defy anyone to say that this headdress looks wrong. I think it looks wonderful, and it teams well with the white flowing bouquet she carried.

The full coronet does not suit every bride (or bridesmaid) but if it does, I think there is nothing better. For one thing, it stays in place more efficiently! You could have a half band for either bride or bridesmaid, and in both cases the first thing to do is to measure the head involved. For a coronet, measure around the top of the head, over the forehead if to be sweeping the face as in the photograph on page 82; if the coronet is to hug the crown of the head, as in the bridesmaid on page 83, measure that circumference instead. For a half band, measure from behind the ears up over the top of the head and down behind the other ear or, much easier, simply use an alice band as a base.

Using a measured piece of good strong florist's wire, build up the equivalent of a garland. Lay the flowers and foliage against the main stem wire and twist, taping with florist's stem tape as the wire revolves. After each two revolutions, place another flower and twist again until you have a long thin garland. Very gently bend the coronet into a circle and wire and tape the ends together. As with any garland, it's the variety of materials used that creates interest – the large bold white flowers of Sara's coronet, or the softer outlines of the bride's headdress in the photograph on page 78.

Bridesmaids' headdresses should of course echo the colourings of the wedding and the bouquet, and should complement the bride's flowers and headdress. The bridesmaid's coronet on page 83 is a slimmer version of the bride's, using smaller artificial flowers, and it has lacy ribbon streamers coming down the back to echo the ribbons on her basket. The half band in the photograph on page 78 is also a slimmer version of the bride's coronet. Yet another type of headdress for a bridesmaid is that on page 86, to accompany the Christmas bouquet. It is made up on a comb and attached firmly to the hair.

In fact, the style and texture of hair of either bride or bridesmaid is a very important consideration, as both affect what types of headdress will be most suitable. I find, for instance, that younger bridesmaids are very difficult as their hair is so fine; when this is the case, I always advise a coronet – at least it stays on top!

A final point about headdresses. Front placements can look good – but think about the view of the congregation. It's the backs of the heads and bodies they will be seeing, so always create interest there. In all the brides' and bridesmaids' headdresses, there is some sort of back interest – the one on page 87 the best of the lot.

BUTTONHOLES AND CORSAGES

Buttonholes are still a part of the main wedding flowers, to be arranged for the principal male guests and family members,

A floral hair decoration for a winter bridesmaid to match the Christmas bouquet on page 74. Made up of holly, ivy, holly berries, and Christmas roses, its ribbon tails match the ribbons in the bouquet.

Never forget to make the back of a headdress interesting – remember that the congregation will have this viewpoint for much of the wedding service.

and should always be included in the budget for the wedding. Many consider white carnations the best – they're certainly traditional – but I like roses better, in white or cream, or even the same rose colour of the bride's bouquet. Whatever you choose, please don't use any fern or silver foil. Keep it as simple as possible!

Corsages – sometimes called sprays – are worn by female guests at a wedding on their dress or suit lapel, pinned on from the back of the fabric. They're in essence a tiny version of a bouquet, and made up similarly. I always give as much thought to these as I do to bouquets and headdresses. Just as with the bride, I like to see a sample of the fabric first: what one lady calls cream, I might not, and think what a confusion there could be over fuchsia pink or donkey brown! When I see the fabric sample, not only is colour clarified, but I can also decide on the weight of the corsage – some materials suit or can hold heavier corsage arrangements. But for some very delicate fabrics, I would avoid pinning flowers on completely, and suggest a handbag spray instead. It's not quite so permanently visible, perhaps, but kinder to your best dress. It's made in the same way as the corsage, and is sized to suit the bag. As I don't like spoiling the front face of the bag by piercing it, I leave a fairly long length of wire and bend it into a hook to press over the open edge of the bag. Don't make this hook too thick as the bag might not close.

FLOWERS FOR WEDDING RECEPTIONS

The flowers for the reception after a wedding, whether at home, in a hotel or a hall of some sort — or even in a marquee — need just as much forward planning as do the flowers in the building where the actual ceremony takes place. Colour schemes need to be echoed, the most effective positions for arrangements will have to be considered well in advance and, if you're like me, you'll want to get involved in all the other celebratory and decorative aspects, such as the table settings and wedding-cake embellishments.

THE ESSENTIAL GROUNDWORK

If a reception is to be small and intimate, for just immediate family and a few friends, then I would suggest that simpler flower decorations such as you would normally have at home are best — turn to page 107 for one idea, or follow some of the ideas in the other sections throughout the book. But if you are going in for a more lavish do, in a much larger area, then this is a different matter altogether, and you can really go to town. Visit the building where the reception is to take place well before the day to plot out your arrangements, noting possibilities for entrances, for the reception room itself. Find out the number of guests expected, the number to be placed on the top table, the number and *type* of tables to be used, etc — and don't forget to discuss your initial ideas with both bride and bridal party and the management of the building. The

An individual table arrangement for a reception, in the green and white colour scheme of a high summer wedding. The candles were the first placements, followed by a star of five pieces of foliage – lady's mantle and ivy – to establish both height and width respectively. The grapes, in three groups, were then fixed in. Dendrobium or Singapore orchids in an interesting citrus green flow to the sides with white spray carnations, white freesias, and small side shoots of 'Bonnie Jean' spray chrysanthemums – which look so much like summer daisies. The main flowers are white 'Tiara' roses (for Yorkshire, of course), and I also used the rose foliage to recess and to hide the mechanics very carefully.

wedding budget still has relevance here, and hotel staff may have to veto some of your ideas if they will hamper access or serving arrangements.

The reception may be in a marquee – an idea that is becoming more popular these days for summer weddings – and one of the major considerations is the colour of the marquee lining. This, hopefully, will have been chosen and ordered by the bride with her general wedding colour scheme in mind – but often this is not so, and you would be amazed at some of the combinations I have had to deal with!

A WELCOMING ARRANGEMENT

Perhaps the most important arrangement to consider – for both hotel and marquee – is that near where the bridal party stand to receive their guests, and near the area where all the guests will be milling after being received. Your flowers must be placed in a position where maximum effect will be gained – and it may also be where the photographer will want to take some pictures, the flowers providing a good backing. The arrangement should be large, and in a position at eye level or above – all the guests will be standing, remember. So many arrangers make the mistake of putting flowers on the floor or on low tables and, as a result, they're never seen. Another favourite place is a fireplace – no fire, so fill the space with an arrangement. As men will always stand with their backs to a fireplace – whether there's a fire or not – all that will be seen of the flowers is the occasional flash of colour through drab-suited legs! A much better position is the mantelshelf itself, where the flowers will at least be visible.

I would prefer to have just one big arrangement – a pedestal perhaps, similar to the one on page 59, or the urn arrangement in the marquee on page 102 – which I would position as near as possible to the receiving line. But often space is limited, and it may be that a hanging arrangement such as that in the church entrance hall on page 55, would be the most suitable. Another 'suspended' idea is an arrangement attached to the foot of a light fitting. The fitting obviously has to be large and secure enough to actually *support* an arrangement, and it should also be high so that the plant material is well above guests' heads, but this can solve many problems in areas such as halls which have limited space and access. The first thing, though, is to seek permission for this sort of decoration: if the hotel is the proud owner of some magnificent chandeliers, they may not take too kindly to you attaching large heavy arrangements to them!

The arrangements can be made in the old-fashioned type of basket that hangs outside many a porch in the summer. Line them first with thin polythene through which the flowers and foliage stems can pass, then fill with soaked floral foam. Lift and fix very fimly into position; therafter, with groundsheet spread out underneath, the arrangement can be done. You might think it's easier to do it *before* hoisting into position, but it's not, as you will find you have too much plant material over the top half of the arrangement, and not enough beneath – where it's more important. For an arrangement like this you will want plenty of foliage (so secure fastening of the basket on to the fitting is *vital*), and after the placement of the flowers, you will need to do a lot of filling in with recessed foliage. I used this idea for the green and white wedding – in the reception room – and added branches of silver birch spreading out to about 2.4 m (8 ft), on which I attached a 'flock' of white doves to tie in with the doves adorning the cake (see below). I also swept artificial garlands between the decorated chandeliers to unify them – and very effective it looked too, transforming the room.

TABLE FLOWERS

Table flower arrangements – important as part of *any* celebration, but vital for a wedding reception – will depend primarily on budget (as always), and can happily vary from the very simplest to the most lavish. They also depend, of course, on the space available, which in turn is ruled by the type of wedding feast that has been ordered. Basically, there are two types: the buffet meal or the sit-down meal. Even buffets can vary though. You could choose a finger-food and glass-balancing occasion, where chairs are at a premium and individual table arrangements aren't really called for: in this case, decorate the light as above (if feasible), the walls or corners, or even the buffet table if there's room (see page 134 for one idea). Or you could have one of those buffets at which, once you have filled your plate, you are all able to sit down at individual tables to eat. If the latter – or if you have chosen to serve a sit-down meal, as I did – table flower arrangements will play a major part in the beauty of the whole occasion.

Once that is decided, the table shapes are the next consideration, as these too will dictate the space available for flowers. You could opt for the long trestle-type tables, with a top table making a U or E shape, with the guests sitting on both sides of the tables; or you could be offered square or oblong individual tables. All these, I think, are more difficult because of the very small amount of room available for you, the flower arranger, after the cutlery, china and glasses have been put in position. With the long tables particularly, all you are left with is a long narrow strip – so what can be done? One solution is the dear old garland once again, placed down the centre of the table, intertwined with narrow, small flowers in the wedding colourings. Another alternative is to do three small narrow arrangements, say, per long table instead of attempting one long one – which could end up looking rather funereal.

I think the best option, though, is round tables, those which will seat from between six to twelve. Whatever number, there is always a reasonable space left in the centre for a good-sized flower arrangement, and I don't think there is anything to beat them both for the finished visual effect and for the ease of the diners. In the photograph on page 91 you can see clearly how super it all looks, and how nothing interferes with anything else: the place settings look good – for 10, an ideal number – and there is enough elbowroom for each guest to eat happily and move freely.

The colourings of the flowers, too, have been chosen, as always, very carefully. You can complement the party room, but if you are following through a flower and colour theme for the whole wedding, you want to continue to complement room *and* bridal party! The individual arrangement shown here is, I think, a good example of that 'togetherness' – a concept you will often come across in this book! With its

A closer look at one of the individual table setting streamers. The satin ribbon is cut into lengths (five for a table for ten, four for eight and so on) that will stretch virtually across the table, pointing to a guest at both ends. They are held in place under the central arrangement, but you can use cellotape as well to make sure, and then weighted down at the fish-tail ends with a tiny arrangement to match those on the napkin rings (see pages 91 and 151). Little rolls of the same ribbon are glued on top as well.

95

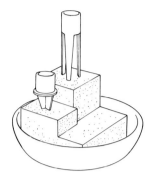

Fixing various types of candle holders into floral foam. Note how the foam is cut so that the candles will be at different levels.

greens and whites, and just a touch of creamy yellow, it echoes the flowers and colourings of the whole high summer wedding theme.

Any central table arrangement must be low and spreading rather than high, so that the guests can see each other and carry on conversations without peering or ducking round sprays of foliage. Always remember, too, that it will be viewed from all sides, so it must be worked in a circle. Here, I used a low flat dish for a container, holding a large piece of soaked floral foam: for not only had I flowers and foliage to place, but candles as well, as this was an evening wedding reception. Incidentally, don't try to use candles during the day – what's the point? – and if you don't want to use candles in an arrangement like this, just visualize feature flowers where the candles are. The first placements were the three candles, held in place with special candle-cup holders – small plastic cups with spikes underneath to push into the floral foam. (If you can't find these – but they should be readily available from a good floral accessories department or local flower shop – tape three cocktail sticks to the bottom of the candle, using floral foam tape, so that half of each stick protrudes beyond the end of the candle; this tripod then acts as 'legs' to push into the floral foam.)

Once the candles are central and stable, the arrangement was started with five pieces of foliage, placed in an almost horizontal position around the dish, like a five-pointed star. This prevents the arrangement from looking square. With candles and these five pieces of foliage, both the height and width of your arrangement are determined. The next stage was to make the bunches of grapes fairly secure. This I did by

To avoid a square look to a central table flower arrangement, place the foliage in a five-pointed star shape.

fixing a piece of florist's stub wire around the end of the 'branch' of the bunch, to make a two-pronged leg which then pushes into the floral foam as would a flower stem. (Do this at this early stage, it's much more difficult later.) I used two sizes of green grapes, large and small for interest, and placed them in three groups around the circular arrangement – and they were real rather than artificial because there are always some guests whose appetites you just can't satisfy!

Now you can carry on round the container with your flowers, keeping to the design already established by the foliage. I also added some white satin ribbon tails, leading out from the arrangement towards each place setting. I thought they were an interesting touch, acting somewhat as a device to bring the whole design of the table together. At the end of each ribbon, cut into fish-tail points, I glued a small group of artificial silk and linen flowers and foliage, which complement those on the napkin rings. Napkin rings are a particular speciality of mine, and I discuss how to make them in greater detail on page 152. They are a simple but extraordinarily effective way of beautifying a table setting.

THE TOP TABLE

This is where you can really go to town as, don't forget, it is the focal point of the whole wedding reception. Everyone's eyes will be fixed on this table – brides are rather like royalty, people can't take their eyes off them! – so you must think of something really interesting. My first plea is please, *please* don't put the cake between the happy couple as happens so often – they've just been joined in holy matrimony, and you

A magnificently decorated table for a magnificently decorated cake. I used artificial flowers and leaves and made them up into circlets for the cake itself, and for the garlands that sweep out across the table top. The cake-top decoration, as I'm sure you'll agree, is rather more interesting than that miniature bride and groom – and any bride could happily keep it for ever as a reminder of her big day.

don't want to split them up already. Make a separate feature of the cake as below.

The first consideration, as usual, is the space available, and the number to be seated there. A top table is usually a long trestle, seating between nine and twelve – but some brides choose that many bridesmaids! As they are seated on one side only, facing the congregation, so to speak, space isn't at quite such a premium as on the guests' tables and, as the guests are facing a white expanse – for the top table will, of course, have a floor-length cloth – you can make a feature of it. The arrangements on the top of the table – roughly one to each three guests along the table, possibly four in all – can flow along and over the table front, softening the table edge. They can also flow to the sides, so that the flowers and foliage form a virtual continuous line along the outer edge of the top table. Don't make them too high, though – guests want to *see* those they've just watched being married – and don't put an arrangement between the couple. Do these arrangements in unison, as you'll get a much better result than if you did one and hoped to get the other three to match.

To drape fabric across a table front—for a wedding top table or cake table perhaps. Once the fabric has been gathered at one end, wired together and pinned, drape, then gather the fabric together with the fingers at the other end. Wire and fix similarly.

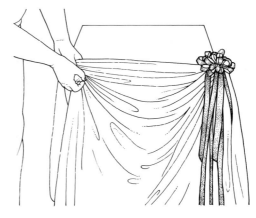

To add an extra special touch to the top table front in my case, guess what turned up – that garland again! It was attached at both corner edges of the table (with drawing pins as it was a trestle) and draped across the front, coming up to meet each downward flow of the table-top arrangements, and crowned with a nice generous ribbon bow with streamers dropping almost to the floor. After it was in place, small flowers were tucked into the garland foliage that matched and linked in with the table-top arrangements. And, to make it an even more fitting focus of all eyes, I arranged much larger groups at the ends of the top table at floor level. A pair of large china dolphins were the containers, with good sized bowls on the top to take the arrangements. These could not be too high, as again the view could not be blocked, so a gentle flowing arrangement was called for. The whole table looked magnificent!

THE CAKE TABLE

Rather than 'divorcing' the couple before their marriage has ever begun by placing the cake between them, I think a wedding cake should be made a special feature all on its own. As in the photograph on page 99, it can sit in solitary splendour on its own table – which can be beflowered, swagged and finished to a highly decorative degree. This is another area where photographs are always taken, so it's an idea worth considering. As with the top table, the cloth goes to the floor (always a good plan, for feet under short-clothed tables can be unattractive and distracting), which makes it look more finished off. This is then swagged with tulle to give a softer effect, gathered at various points – where the cake-encircling arrangements sweep out – and caught with ribbon bows. Nestling in these were white doves, which linked up with the doves on the cake-top decoration and those escapees on the light-fitting garlands described on page 93.

As I'm not too keen on those pillars which hold up various cake levels, leaving gaps in between cakes, we chose a succession of cake layers which rested directly on the layer below, and I chose to make a feature of these areas with some floral decorations. The maker of the cake had fashioned some magnificent icing roses on each level – to hide the joins – so I constructed very delicate and small garlands from artificial materials to wind in between these. The effect of the dark green foliage and white flowers on the sheer gleaming white of the royal icing was magnificent. I also made garland-type arrangements on the table top, around the bottom layer of the cake, which swept out at points to the edge of the table.

I then created a cake-top decoration that many would consider 'over the top' – but it's a focal point, so why not make a show....I use artificial flowers always, so the cake doesn't get damp – and the bride has a magnificent reminder to keep for ever (Sara's cake-top extravaganza is now displayed under a Victorian glass dome). For this sort of arrangement, tiny and delicate, a very small container is needed and, to let you into one of my little secrets, I use the white plastic tops of aerosol cans (waste not, want not, I say), which do a very good job. I first concocted a branch for the doves to perch on, by covering lengths of florist's stub wire with white stem tape, leaving a double prong of wire at the end to help it stand properly in the styrofoam. The doves

*A marquee welcome arrangement in a large garden urn overflowing with the joys of
a summer wedding. The foliage is ruscus and western hemlock to create height and
width; the flowers are Bristol fairy, irises, white and yellow carnations with yellow
and white lilies to give weight to the centre. The artificial garlands are decorated
with Bristol fairy, white roses and yellow satin ribbon bows.*

A 'ball tree' makes an interesting welcome decoration in a marquee – or anywhere else for that matter. It looks as if it is suspended in mid air, but the trunk is a broom handle set in concrete in a plant pot. The foliage is box, and the flowers, pushed into a nail-secured block of floral foam, are carnations, and spray carnations, an interesting single-spray chrysanthemum, and a lovely blossom called bouvardia. To lighten the outline, I used the old favourite Bristol fairy, and curled streamers of pink ribbon sweep downwards to complement the festooning of the marquee lining.

were then attached, and the branch placed before the arrangement proper was begun. As the cake would be viewed from all sides, the arrangement had to be done accordingly. Another 'theme' of the wedding was a 'pearly' one – with pearls on the bride's dress and in the bouquet – and pearls were introduced also into the cake top. They come in sprays on nylon wires and can be bought in any good florists' or flower accessories department – and they bring a lot of movement and life into any group. Sprays of lily of the valley and blossom and tiny white roses were the flowers, contrasting beautifully with the dark green foliage.

MARQUEE FLOWERS

This is the other large area in which a wedding reception can take place, and what could be nicer on a glorious summer's day. (Not so enjoyable on a blustery spring or autumn afternoon or evening when the canvas starts a-flapping, and those terrible blow heaters are switched on!)

Again, as with any wedding, it's all a matter of being organized in advance. As I said, the first consideration is that of the marquee lining colour. I always try to get a piece of the lining material so that I know what I'm dealing with. From experience over the years, I have found that it's always better to go for slightly darker shades of the bridal colour scheme: if the latter is pale pink, say, go for a slightly deeper pink for the flowers. This is mainly because of the amount of light which comes into a marquee, which can 'bleach' colours just as much as the light coming through a church window.

If there is room, have a welcoming arrangement near to the

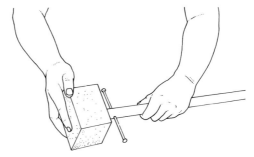

To make a ball tree, hammer in 4 nails (2 will often do), and wedge on a piece of floral foam. The nails will prevent the foam slipping down the pole.

entrance. On page 102, a garden urn on a small table holds a profusion of summer flowers. It is big, bold and exciting, and would be a wonderful background for some photographs. Do make sure it is absolutely stable, though. The garlands above solve the problem of what to do when you want to use flowers near to the edge of the marquee, where top and sides meet and where it is so low. As usual the basic garland was hung first (when fresh, it can be kept damp in polythene for quite some time if made well in advance). Then and only then, will you be able to see where flowers and/or other decorations should be placed. Here I have used plenty of ribbon as I think it's very effective – yellow to match the flowers below and the marquee lining – with simple placements of fresh Bristol fairy and white roses.

As a complete contrast – but an idea that also welcomes (anywhere and at any time of the year) – you could make a ball tree. These are very easy as long as you get the mechanics right. A broom handle is anchored into a large plant pot filled with cement and both pot and handle are painted a pale shade of green (you could also paint the 'earth' brown if you liked). About 7.5 cm (3 inches) from the top of the broom handle, knock in four 7.5 cm (3 inch) nails at N, S, E and W, upon which you can anchor a half block of floral foam, soaked first and then wrapped in clingfilm to keep it together and moist. You then simply go round the block completing a ball shape, firstly with foliage and then with flowers. Box foliage is good for this type of arrangement as it fills in so well, and once you have placed your flowers, be very generous with ribbon bows and streamers. Ribbon isn't expensive and it looks so good. To curl the ends of the ribbon

A marquee pole festooned with flat-backed baskets of flowers – two here, on one pole, but you can use as many as taste and budget dictate. After the outline plant material – ruscus and western hemlock – was placed into the floral foam, the large bows of satin ribbon were secured. Stocks, white and yellow carnations and 'Bonnie Jean' spray chrysanthemums bring weight into the arrangement, while the outline, as with the yellow marquee welcoming arrangement, is lightened by Bristol fairy.

*For a smaller wedding reception – one at home perhaps – a large massed flower arrangement, here centrally positioned in a sitting room, would be ideal. I wanted to use all the summer glories, and chose a large Victorian alabaster urn (with an internal liner dish) as the raised and impressive container. The outline was created by broom, Bristol fairy, ruscus and western hemlock. Then, once I'd acquired my desired shape, I worked in the flowers from all sides (it's central, so to be viewed from all around, remember): lilies (*longiflorum*) carnations, gerberas, alstroemeria, roses and sprays of pink orchids with, as a filling-in flower, two-tone spray chrysanthemums. Although this is a large arrangement, it still looks light.*

107

– to make it look more interesting – draw the ribbon tightly and quickly along the back of a knife and it will spring into curls. You will also see, on page 103, that I have used the same ribbon to make a tie-back for the marquee lining.

The classic decoration in a marquee, though, is some sort of arrangement on the poles – the things that hold the marquee up! What you can do depends entirely on how the erectors have done their job. Some firms tidy the poles where the guy ropes have been finished off with a fanned-out shape basket, point to the base and fan shape to the top. This can take various containers into which arrangements can be made, but they must be very large to look good, with plenty of height and flow to the sides. If small tight groups are arranged in these containers, they give the impression that they're slipping down inside the fan shape! Garlands can also be wound round the poles which can look very effective, but as you need very long lengths, allow time for preparation.

Hanging baskets can also be used – and they do look good – but another idea that I have come up with is flat-backed baskets (looking just like old bicycle baskets) which I attach to the poles at various heights. I much prefer these to the traditional hanging basket as they sit flat against the pole and stay in position even in the strongest of gales when all else is on the move! As they're rather an odd shape, it's difficult to find an appropriate internal container, so I line the baskets first with very thick polythene and then wedge in soaked floral foam. If you don't think it's quite your scene to be up and down a ladder with each couple of flowers – relax. The arrangements can be done on the table and then lifted into position when finished. See page 106.

Smaller Wedding Receptions

The flower arrangements discussed above are all for larger gatherings, but thought must also be given to small receptions, given in the home perhaps. There are a couple of factors to take into consideration. The first is the style of the home: if traditional, arrange your flowers traditionally; if modern, then something simple and dramatic would be the answer. The colourings of the room you choose for your arrangement are important too – as always! – and your flowers must be chosen to be complementary. You could choose welcome arrangements, staircase garlands, hanging baskets – any of the ideas discussed throughout the book, but scaled down to 'home size' – or you could just concentrate your flower power in one principal area such as a central table in a sitting room as in the photograph on page 107. Make sure as always that the flowers will be *seen* when guests are milling to and fro, and also try to remember to leave as much surface space as possible for guests to put things on.

Two points to make about this arrangement. Firstly, the container is alabaster and you must always remember that this material is porous, so needs a liner container for water. I once saw a lovely alabaster Venus de Milo figurine being used at a flower show. The competitor had placed the base of the figurine in water – and by the following day, not only was she without arms, but was down to her knees in a rather cloudy pool! The second point concerns the use of orchids. In a massed flower arrangement such as this, the stems of orchids are often not long enough, so don't just stuff them into the arrangement, they will be wasted. Many orchid sprays come with a plastic or glass tube containing water at the end of their stems. If you haven't kept them, ask the florists if they have any spare – or simply buy glass test tubes. Tape the test tube to a thin garden cane, fill the tube with water, and place the cane into the arrangement as if it were another flower. The orchid is then placed in the water in the test tube.

PRESENTATION THANK-YOUS

It has become quite a tradition after a wedding for the couple to give their parents a gift to say thank-you – and what better than flowers! You could, of course, take the easy way out and present both sets of parents with a bouquet in cellophane with large silken bows – but I'm not really in favour of this. Quite apart from anything else, it means that, once the flowers are taken home, they have to be 'dismantled' from their wrappings and put in water – and then of course they would have to be arranged. Rather than giving the parents – usually the mother – a job to do so soon after the wedding, why not give the thank-you presentation flowers already arranged!

My idea opposite utilizes a very interesting basket made of bound twigs which comes from the Far East and gives a natural look to any arrangement. The basket has two divisions, so into one I placed a plastic container – a margarine box, in fact – and filled it with a good-sized piece of floral foam that would keep the flowers going for a long time. Here I used gerbera, spray carnations and Bristol fairy with lovely sprays of Singapore orchids, and bows of velvet ribbon. To please the fathers, I added a bottle of champagne to the other basket division – a nice memento of an exciting day!

In order to express their gratitude to their parents, young newlyweds traditionally give them presents — and what nicer than a pretty basket flower arrangement with the additional cheer of a bottle of champagne. In one division of the twig basket I made an arrangement using gerberas, spray carnations and Bristol fairy, with lovely delicate sprays of Singapore orchids. I added a bow of velvet ribbon to the flower half and then another to the bottle of champagne. Something for both Mum and Dad — cheers!

111

FLOWERS FOR PARTIES

In the first chapter I described how you can extend a welcome with flowers all over your home. In this chapter, I shall concentrate more specifically on parties – on table arrangements for spring and summer dinner and buffet parties, on side table and welcoming splendours for autumn celebrations, and on individual occasions such as wedding anniversaries, coming of age and children's birthday parties.

PARTIES THROUGHOUT THE YEAR

Although it may seem too obvious to state, the four seasons of the year are of vital importance to the flower arranger. The flowers and foliages readily available vary from season to season and I think we should always try to concentrate as much as possible on the flowers that *naturally* belong to that season, that we naturally *associate* with that season. Nowadays, of course, when you look at the blooms in florists' shops, the seasons would seem to be overlapping, with so much material being flown in from all ends of the earth. I can't complain about this in the least (in *my* business!), but when someone produces daffodils that bloom in July, I'm giving up! I was once asked on an Australian TV programme what I thought was the main difference between flower arranging in Britain and Australia, and my answer was the four distinct seasons that we in the northern hemisphere can enjoy. There I saw spring bulbs flowering in the same beds as roses – which looked very comical, I thought!

Parties can be held at all times throughout the year, so I

think you should try and reflect the 'feel' of the seasons in your party arrangements, whether for the centre of a dinner table or for a side table. In spring, for instance, the essence of the season is freshness and lightness after the gloom of winter. It is a lovely time of year, although flowers are not cheap. The answer is to use your imagination in order to make the most of an expensive few – which I have done in the two spring dinner table arrangements on pages 114 and 115. In summer, you have a much greater choice of plant materials, so you can create what you like. Summer is warm (we hope) and colourful – so choose flowers and arrangements to reflect those qualities. The crisp charm of the small summer arrangement on page 118 could bedeck a patio or conservatory dinner table – or serve for a *diner à deux* in a bedsit, or small dining cum sitting room.

There are a number of things to remember about dinner table flowers. One is that they mustn't be too overpowering – the table could easily look cluttered. Neither must there be any gaps in your arrangements, for these are more closely viewed than all others: as you don't want your guests to see any mechanics, go round carefully, tucking small pieces of recessed foliage well in. Follow the 'rules' outlined for the wedding table flower arrangement to keep to a good shape (see page 96). Colour is important too, and the flowers can and should reflect the colours of your tablecloth, napkins, china, cutlery etc, the room itself even – togetherness! In the picture on page 114, the pinks and creams of the room are echoed in the flowers and the pale pinks of the candles and napkins, and set off by the china with its gold edge. In all the other dinner table arrangements, you can see the ideas behind

The spring-like combination of pink and cream here is fresh and interesting, chosen to reflect the colourings of the room, and emphasized by the use of pale pink candles and napkins. On a fabric-covered base, in a simple plastic dish with soaked floral foam, the candles were the first placements. After arranging the foliage, nephrolepis fern in a five pointed star – the 'rule' for central table arrangements – the fruit, green grapes and Granny Smith apples, were placed in three groups, unanchored just in case anyone fancied a nibble! Cream freesias flow to the sides following the foliage lines, with a very interesting anemone-centred spray chrysanthemum, pale to deep pink. To bring the whole colour scheme together, I found a spray carnation that was both cream and pink – and with the addition of cream ivy leaves, the arrangement was complete.

114

In a spring table setting I have used two round Italian ceramic dishes — which even look wonderful displayed empty. To get the two levels, I supported the top dish with a cut-down plastic refrigerator box, then two floral foam saucers were placed at the two different levels. As usual, I did the arrangement from all sides, but worked them together as if one arrangement were divided in half. Nephrolepis fern is the outline foliage, and freesias were the first flower placements, followed by the lovely golden yellow roses. Roses like their own foliage used, so that was the second foliage placement. Instead of another large flower — which would have made the arrangement too heavy looking — I added the lightness of the useful spray chrysanthemum, here side pieces of a spider variety. With the white china and cutlery on the yellow napkin, the whole colour scheme is emphasized.

To make a simple base for hanging flowers for drying, place an old piece of garden trellis over garden canes fixed to the ceiling. Gather the flowers into bunches and suspend on wire hooks from the trellis.

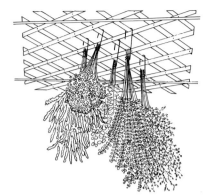

the colour scheme. Containers, too, can be anything and everything, ranging from those round ceramic dishes on page 115 to a plastic dish, when the container won't be seen. It's a theme I constantly reiterate, but do look around your possessions: I'm sure many people have got wonderful things that have never seen the light of day as a flower container. Don't forget, if it holds water it will hold flowers – and even if it won't hold water, like the ceramic dishes on page 115, you can adapt them and *add*, so that they will still fulfil the desired function. Don't be afraid either of using 'accessories', if appropriate, in table flower arrangements: the Dresden figures on page 118 add immeasurably to the design – and the birds on page 119 – a couple from a now extensive bird collection – were the actual inspiration for the arrangement.

For autumn entertaining, once more echo the mood and feel of this wonderful season – mists, mellow fruitfulness and all. It's an ideal time for utilizing preserved or dried plant material, and their muted colours echo the browns, oranges and reds of the trees outside. Over the years I have collected dried plant materials from all over the world. The sea grape leaves on page 119 come from the tropics, and travel well on the way home, packed flat in the suitcase bottom. The gnarled grape vine cuttings on page 122 come from France: I just happened to be passing a field and there they were – never miss an opportunity! The wood roses on page 119 grow wild in many parts of the world and, as they're rather more brittle, they should be carried home in something like an old shoe box – I never travel without one for that reason!

Many plants and plant materials can be preserved at home, however, I won't go into too much detail here – but for the

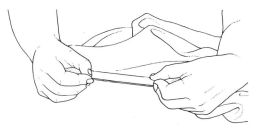

To make a covered base, lay the fabric edges against the glued edge of the fibreboard shape, and stretch, press and pin into place.

greatest drying success, there's nothing to beat hanging flowers and plants in a light, dry and airy place and letting them dry naturally. Gourds as in the picture on page 119 are easy to dry – and can be bought dried – as are the pomegranates. Don't ever pierce them with wire stems before they're thoroughly dried though, or they'll simply mould away.

You can still use fresh materials in autumn, but you can mix them with dried for interesting combinations – and adding fresh fruit, as on page 122, adds even more visual and textural excitement. As the arrangement here was high, I needed to add weight to the bottom, and I used water, half filling the ewer (plastic not stone!). Many people would use sand, pouring it into the container, but this can be messy and hard to clean later: if I want to use sand, I put it in a plastic bag closed with a twist-tie. The ewer has a very narrow top, and it's worth repeating (I did this with church vases, you might remember) that the floral foam is cut into a wedge shape, narrow end into the container, and all the thicker plant materials were given thin wire stems.

This group, too, sits on a base covered with hessian, and I shall outline briefly how to make these. Cut fibreboard to the size and shape required then cut a piece of fabric to fit, with a little extra all round. Put quick-drying glue on the side edges of the board and lay the fabric on top, pulling and pressing it to lie flat over the top and to adhere tightly to the glue. Push dressmakers' pins at intervals into the glued edges to hold the material firm. Trim the edges well once the glue has dried, and cover the pinned and glued edges with some braid to finish. You can make an amazing and varied number of bases

This crisp navy and white setting for a summer diner à deux *looks very welcoming – or is it that glass of wine? The container is a Victorian lifted sugar dish with, dancing around its base, looking as if they were part of it, the Dresden 'four seasons'. Into the top of a tall piece of floral foam I fixed a couple of lovebirds on a branch, made of Parian ware, an unglazed pottery. A simple arrangement was then built up into the remaining floral foam, using the summery daisy shapes of 'Bonnie Jean' spray chrysanthemums, Bristol fairy – in which nestles the odd white rose – and trails of ivy. A simple little setting for a simple little dinner party.*

For an autumnal party piece – perhaps for a party after huntin', shootin' or fishin' – I was inspired by a pair of fan-tailed doves from China, made of natural plant materials. They sit on a rough hessian-covered base. As I wanted round fruity shapes, I added bunches of pine and mahogany grapes – bought in the United States – which were anchored to a piece of styrofoam taped on to a large weighted pinholder. The dried gourds and pomegranates add to the 'fecundity' of the group. The wonderful shape of sea grape leaves adds texture and colour, and the wood roses, gathered in the West Indies, with bean pods, mahogany pods and dried cactus, contribute interest and height.

119

like this, to suit individual settings and colour schemes. All kinds of bases add immeasurably to the look of a grouping: the circle of mirror glass on page 127 brings the whole shimmering group together, and cake boards on page 130 act as base for both arrangement and place setting.

THANKSGIVING PARTIES

While on the subject of autumnal parties and autumnal flower arranging, why not consider celebrating Thanksgiving? This, like Christmas to the British flower arranger, must be the favourite celebratory occasion for American flower arrangers. (In fact *I* love Christmas so much I've missed winter out of the seasonal section above, and am giving it a distinct section all of its own.) Thanksgiving is the fourth Thursday in November, commemmorating the arrival of the Pilgrims in the New World, and their first harvest. It's the equivalent of the British harvest festival, but is *much more* special, with American families coming together to celebrate in unison, with a special meal of roast turkey, pumpkin pie etc.

Even if you're not American, it's a wonderful excuse for a party, and I think a welcome could be extended right from the beginning with a ring such as that on page 123. This is something I do particularly at Christmas, with holly, red bows, red berries, the lot – but there's no reason why the idea shouldn't be utilized at other times of year. The colourings here are distinctly autumnal – so for Thanksgiving or a bonfire party perhaps – but it could also be used for a children's party instead of those groups of balloons pinned to a front door. An idea anyway. It looks colourful and cheerful

Door-rings come in many sizes, and are made of many different types of plant materials.

Tape (or wire) a piece of styrofoam on to a door ring to take an arrangement.

and your guests will start to enjoy themselves even before they step into the house!

Inside the house for Thanksgiving, I would do something quite different, as in the picture on page 126. We all have our own ideas of what we want to do and live with (and that includes me), but I don't like *too* many things dotted about. What I *do* like, though, is to show it off, all splendidly together, as here. If you cram everything together, not only does it look generous and exciting, but there will be room left on other surfaces for the guests to put things down. If, for instance, this grouping in the picture was put on a dresser in your hall, what a wonderful additional welcome it would be for your guests. But don't be *too* lavish with your ingredients: these groupings should always have togetherness, things of a type that look as though they were meant to go together – basketry, wood and old stone pots. All natural looking and autumnal in feel.

The first thing I did in this case was to take off the back of the dresser – it wasn't fixed on anyway – because the plain wall was a better foil for the grouping. This may look rather small at first glance, but when I tell you that the large wicker

121

*Above: This autumn welcome ring, made of natural bound twigs, has a wired-on
piece of styrofoam at the foot, into which the arrangement is made. Wheat sprays
with dried Australian ferns make the outline, poppy heads and dried gourds give
interest to the shape. Glossy red and yellow artificial fruits and red American silk
ribbons add deep colour and, so that the ring doesn't look too monotone, two sprays
of variegated spider plant in silk add a different colour and texture. One simple
idea which you could vary infinitely.*

*Left: For a fresh autumnal arrangement in a weighted ewer — made of plastic,
although it looks like stone — I used ruscus and eucalyptus sprays as outline foliage.
Both were given stems of thin wire to fit into the floral foam wedged in the narrow
top of the ewer. Spray carnations with their nice gentle flowing action were placed
into the sides and top, with a little ivy. The central flowers are orange carnations
and 'Enchantment' lilies, with recessed bronze spray chrysanthemums. Around the
base, to add texture, interest and colour, are grape vine cuttings, and a selection of
fruit — pineapples, grapes, apples and oranges.*

123

disc is over 1.25 m (4½ ft) in diameter, you will, I am sure, get an idea of the scale of the setting. This meant, of course, that I needed a *lot* of other material to fill in the 'picture' and, as you can see, I used a lot! It's busy, I admit, but I cannot stress enough that this sort of grouping should look generous, exciting and above all colourful.

WEDDING ANNIVERSARY PARTIES

Any wedding anniversary is an occasion to celebrate, and because they are represented popularly by 'colours', they are tailor-made for the enthusiastic flower arranger. The two that stand out more than others, though, are the silver and golden, twenty-five and fifty respectively, and I *love* using those two colours in arrangements.

In the silver arrangement on page 127, I have used artificial silver materials (obviously) with fresh pink flowers – a non-traditional combination perhaps, but it is nice and has proved extremely popular. To get the wonderful silvery effect, I used a variety of materials which are a little more unusual. The base is a circle of mirror glass, available in many sizes from your local do-it-yourself shop, and I thought this a rather nice idea as, with the crystal and glass, the whole arrangement would shimmer. The two main placements are two different sized, star-shaped dishes from Dartington Glass, made in such a way that they almost look as if they had been sprayed with silver paint. The floral foam is in another glass dish *between* these two to take the arrangement – thus allowing the star dishes to be revealed in all their glory. Along with the dull silver lurex leaves (wire mounted into sprays of foliage), the mirror fruit and silver grapes and baubles, I also half filled the star dishes with handfuls of shattered windscreen (windshield) glass. Shattered windscreen (windshield) glass, I hear you exclaim? It's interesting, tiny shards with many sides which gleam and twinkle, and it's not difficult to handle. All you have to do to obtain it is to go along to your local friendly garage, plastic bag in hand – and ask!

A golden wedding is such a special time – the achievement of the great 50 years together – and many people would organize a local hall or hotel and do all the celebrating in one go. Other couples, though – and golden wedding celebrants *are* around seventy at least – might prefer to have one or two smaller gatherings in their own home. At large parties, it's often very difficult to get round everybody; at a couple of smaller parties the two concerned could at least move around and be sure that they've spoken to the majority of their friends.

Thus I designed the golden scheme to suit various times of day – lunch, tea or dinner time perhaps. The basic table-centre flower arrangement on page 130 is made into a low dish set on golden cakeboards glued together. For a celebration during the day, you simply remove the candlesticks – the arrangement looks quite happy without – and for evening they are inserted at the sides, the gold candles are lit, and then, in this case, covered with glass storm candle galleries. (The candlesticks are Victorian glass, the ones that come with those dressing-table sets, but the galleries are modern, replacement shades for chandeliers from a well-known, large chain store!)

The gold-encrusted place mats could be used at any time of

A massed welcome grouping for autumn. In the centre of a large wicker disc I placed an artificial leaf welcome ring encrusted with massed red baubles and fruits. From the beam I fixed an artificial garland which is again massed with things made from corn – bells, rings and hearts – interspersed with red fruits, ribbon bows and natural pine cones. On the left of the dresser top itself, I arranged some traditional winter foliage and berries, with a ribbon bow and spilling fruit to give good weight and balance to the cider jars and wine collection on the right. (Whether you still have balance when the bottles are emptied is another story!) To keep the scene going, I have also included some extras – strings of onion and garlic, a jar full of wooden spoons and two pottery lanterns carrying candles, just to add that twinkle.

For a silver wedding anniversary, I made an arrangement into a small dish between
two beautiful glass star dishes on top of a circle of mirror glass. The dull silver
lurex leaves made the outline foliage, then I secured in some wonderful silver
bunches of glass grapes. Pale pink Singapore orchids flow to the sides and create
the height, and then I placed a band of pink bridal roses across the arrangement.
Small sprays of Bristol fairy lighten the outlines. To avoid that rather up and
down look, I added cross-wise silver baubles, fruits covered in tiny mirrors, and
strings of glass beads – with shattered windscreen (windshield) glass in the star
dishes!

the day, perhaps most effectively in the evening. I was excited by this idea, which came to me while planning this book, and it could be wonderfully effective at any time of year. Just think of Christmas – gold or silver cake boards with red and green festive fruit and foliage edges! What started me off was the cake board base for the main arrangement, two thin gold cake boards of different sizes glued together (there's a 2.5 cm/1 inch difference between them). I used the same for the place mats, and that inch of size difference was where I glued on the various selected gold-coloured bits and pieces. Some things I spray-painted with gold, some were already that colour. As always with something like this, it's the different textures and varieties of tones that make it more interesting. I started by glueing on a layer of different leaf and fern shapes – the foliage first, just as in an arrangement. Do let these dry thoroughly before glueing on the next items, here the tiny gold baubles and fruit shapes. A wonderful idea, I think and so celebratory! Don't forget, though, to echo the colours in all the other table accessories: a gold cloth, gold-edged china and napkins (in a golden napkin ring, perhaps, see page 152), gold cutlery and golden champagne – the complete golden touch!

For a more formal sitting or living room – or indeed a hall, if it were big enough – you could try something like the gold extravaganza on page 131. This re-emphasizes one of the major concepts of flower arranging in the home: your arrangement must be chosen to match your room. This gleaming festooning would be quite out of place in a small or rustic room, while here, on a marble-topped console table, with a gilded mirror as backdrop, it looks stunning. I use this setting most of the time for a flower arrangement, but this gilded magnificence looks wonderfully festive for a golden anniversary party – and it could of course be an idea for Christmas as well.

I like arrangements against mirrors, but we don't seem to do this much in the UK. People often shy away from artificial plant materials too, such as are used here, but I can't for the life of me understand why. It's what you do with the materials that matters and they're so glorious these days. Here, in the principal table-top arrangement, in styrofoam in a heavyweight container, you can see I've really gone to town with my golds. For any arrangement such as this, you must first think of colour – the secret of success lies in using various hues and shades of gold, never just the one uninteresting tone. The next thing to consider is different surfaces and textures; if everything were bright and shiny, it would again be rather uninteresting. As a result, the focal point has been created with many shades and textures – the gold silk roses, the glass baubles and the lurex spirals.

The first placements, though, as in any flower arrangement, are the foliages, of stemmed artificial fern and leaf sprays. These are bought with straight stems (I have even seen them *arranged* straight), but it is so simple – and one of their main advantages – to give the stems a softer line by just running them through your fingers. Once the height and width of the arrangement have been delineated, create your focal point with features just as you would in a fresh flower arrangement. The lurex spirals are easy to place as are the silk roses. You will have to make 'stems' for the gold glass baubles. Beside the metal cap and hanger of the bauble there is also a hole, and

A magnificent golden table setting for a golden wedding celebration – with home-made gold place mats. The central flower arrangement can be adapted for display with or without the candles and galleries. Into a low container on the double cake board, nephrolepis ferns create the outline. Gold freesias, favourites with ladies who have reached this golden time, flow to the edges and create the height: a difficulty when the candlesticks are to be 'in and out', but the one top flower was a happy medium. Gradually coming down from the top placements are pale gold roses to fill the main part of the arrangement. All it needed finally was a few single flowers of a spray chrysanthemum, tucked in both to hide the mechanics and to give yet another flower shape.

*On a marble-topped console table with a gilded mirror as backdrop, I have created
a gold extravaganza made entirely of artificial materials. The principal table-top
arrangement is made with a varied selection of bought gilded fern and leaf sprays,
with glass baubles, lurex spirals and gold silk roses as the main features. A pair
of large church candlesticks are a nice accompaniment to the group, and to make
the setting even more splendid, I swung lurex garlands from gilded brackets – with
cherub-encrusted pennants – to a central cluster of baubles supporting a gilded
welcome ring. Smaller arrangements sit atop the brackets to give a complete
linkage to the whole setting.*

into this I force a slim wooden skewer, just until it reaches the other side of the bauble. I then secure the skewer to the metal ring hanger with floral foam tape. When pushing the bauble stem into the arrangement, always hold the stem rather than the bauble to prevent the skewer bursting through.

The baubles in the central top of the grouping are stemmed and then taped together and attached to the relevant part of the mirror, with the ring – made of gold tinsel and baubles pushed into a bought styrofoam ring suspended below. The dual top arrangements were made into small pieces of styrofoam, working both together, and then taped with floral foam tape to the brackets holding the pennants. Once this grouping is complete, you will not need any other arrangement in the room, as I'm sure you can appreciate! It's a classic example of all one's eggs in one basket!

COMING OF AGE PARTIES

I'm not quite sure when coming of age is these days, at 18 or 21 – and suspect we're kept guessing because young people would like two parties instead of one! But whether they're now able to vote or to use the key of the door, it's an occasion to celebrate, and one on which to use celebratory flowers. Whether you are partying at home or in a hall or hotel, you can design something beautiful to make the whole thing more festive. For small gatherings, there are many ideas throughout the book you could adapt; for a larger one, with a long buffet table, say, you could try something like I've done in the picture on page 134. I've started with the ladies, so it's all in pink. (See drawing on page 98 too.)

The table is the first priority at a buffet party and, unless space is at a premium, don't push it into a corner out of the way. Show it off. It's best if guests can use all sides – to facilitate the serving of the food – but if it has to be one-sided, don't worry. Whichever, you want to dress it up to the hilt (according to expense, of course). I found some yardage of fabric which was the right price and very drapeable – infinitely preferable to plain white damask at a less formal occasion like this. It covered the top and sides and came to floor level. As they were trestle tables, I was able to gather and drape separate yardages along the front: catch with a length of florist's wire, twist into a ring under the head of a drawing pin and push it home. I would have used large ribbon bows at these gathered points, but as I had some flowers left over from the main flower arrangement, I made a separate end of table arrangement into a pew-end box (as used for the wedding, see page 48). These could have hung down the front of the table, but I sat them on the table top with just the ribbons falling down the front.

Although these latter flowers are at food level, in general I think that flowers for a buffet table should be high up – preferably about 55 cm (22 inches) from the table top – and *away* from the food. Finding the right sort of container, though, can be difficult – but that used here only goes to show how the flower arranger's eye can pick up the possibilities of even the most out-of-the-ordinary thing. In a gifty seaside shop, I found a pair of floor-standing ashtrays of glass with metal strips, and the top part for the ash takes the floral foam for an arrangement. I don't smoke, but I love these ashtrays!

It's easy to think up ideas for girls' parties, but not so

Buffet table ideas for a girl's coming of age party. The main table-top arrangement is made into floral foam wedged into the ash part of a floor-standing ashtray! The long candles are the first placements, and as they increase the height of the arrangement, gentle flowing lines were called for. Ruscus foliage together with some commercially bought Australian heath foliage gave me the delicate outline I wanted. Pale pink spray carnations followed this shape, and echoed the colours of the main carnations in the centre of the arrangement. Tucked-in pieces of spray chrysanthemum and bouvardia finish it off, with a few large ivy leaves to hide any mechanics. The same flowers are used, with the addition of pink satin ribbon bows and streamers, in the 'pew-end' arrangement on the corner of the table.

*It might seem daunting to design an arrangement for a boy's coming of age party,
but ingenuity has always been the prime characteristic of the flower arranger. On
red place mats I arranged two plastic long-playing record holders, one lifted on a
square metal frame, re-sprayed black. It was easy to wedge containers into the
three divisions of the holders to take the fresh plant materials – red gerberas and
carnations. I hid the mechanics with some dried leaves, sprayed black. The small
top and large central placing is dried giant hogweed, also sprayed black, which
easily wedged into the containers. Any lad would appreciate this drama!*

simple when it comes to the boys. Many might think that boys wouldn't like flowers – but of course they do, they just don't want anything too pretty-pretty. I think boys need a bit of drama, and strong colours, so on went the thinking cap to find the right containers. In the picture on page 135, you should be able to see that I have used two dramatic black containers which are plastic holders for long-playing records! You see how ingenious we have to be? And I think you must agree that the result is splendid. The reds and blacks, good masculine colours, are echoed by the black and white mattress ticking for the cloth, by the red place mats under the arrangement, by the black place mats and red napkins. A true togetherness!

CHILDREN'S PARTIES

Children's parties have always been a great joy to me. It's a long time since I organized parties for my daughter Sara, as you can appreciate (she got married in the second chapter of this book!), but I hope to have grandchildren's parties to think about some time in the future. I know that many people think that it's a waste of time organizing anything too special, or involving too much effort and expense, for children – but I just can't agree. You, as arranger/mother/whatever will have enormous fun, and the kids – not as philistine as everyone thinks – will appreciate it all thoroughly.

For a start, the expense is, in most cases, minimal. Just look round in the stationery departments of the large stores and you will see the most wonderful array of paper items just waiting to be used for a party – and think of avoiding all that washing up afterwards. And for any parents who have been sensible enough to deliver themselves of children in the summer months, an outside party is ideal, and just right for all sorts of decoration. My daughter was, very conveniently, born in July, and I used to come up with all sorts of ideas, always very colourful – lots of balloons, cellophane bags of sweets hanging from the trees, lollipop bushes in the borders etc. For a boy's party on a canal boat the other day, I created a completely blue boat, all the throw-away items were blue – and about fifty blue balloons bobbed behind in the breeze. There are *so* many things you can do – and I hope the two ideas here will give you many more.

The little girl's party decoration on page 139 came together very easily. I already had the two fine wicker cone umbrella shapes: I'd found them in Spain in a local market, and the idea was to use them at a christening filled with sugared almonds (traditional in many European countries). I hadn't used them in fact, but when I came across the paper parasols – so cheap, they were almost giving them away – I knew that, using them together, I had the basis for my arrangement. To echo the wicker cones, I used wicker bases – like those used in the background of the Thanksgiving massed arrangement, all light and summery in feel and colour. This arrangement could be centrally placed on a table, with other small tables dotted about in the garden bearing the edible goodies.

Another idea for a party such as this would be to make cellophane cornets of sweets, tied at the top with pink ribbon bows and decorated with those tiny parasols you get in posh cocktails. Hang these from nearby trees and you've decorated the garden to match the central arrangement – and, needless

Above: A bright and cheerful home-made Christmas cracker bursting with colourful – and largely edible – goodies, for the centre of a children's Christmas party tea table. The 'explosion' contains small crackers, plaster buttons, sticks of rock and candy, sweet-filled boxes and interesting plastic fruit and vegetable shapes. Some bows of ribbon and a few streamers finish it off to perfection. With a red cloth and festive paper plates, anyone – not just a child – would be delighted to sit here!

Right: For a girl's party, this parasol arrangement would be perfect. I strapped a low tray to the basketwork base for security, and the first placements into the soaked floral foam were the paper parasols, their handles lengthened by the use of thin garden canes. The wicker umbrella cones went in next, with pink ribbon bows and various decorative items – silk flowers and ribbons – attached to their handles. Summer flowers wind their way through the lower half of the group: spray and large carnations, and Bristol fairy interspersed with mixed summer garden foliage.

To make the bursting cracker effect, cut outwards with sharp scissors from a central incision. A piece of styrofoam placed inside takes the arrangement.

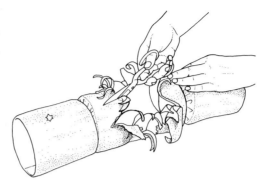

to say, each little girl gets to take one home with her! This is a much better idea, I think, than a chunk of cake carried home in a hot, sweaty hand. The hanging present idea would be very easy to carry out at any other time of year, for inside. You could make up a ball tree (see page 105) while edible goodies mounted on to stems, or even a bare branch wedged into a heavy pot and decorated would still look good.

The other fantastic time for a children's party is, of course, Christmas. (In fact, it's a great time for a party *whatever* your age!) Use paper items again – there is a huge selection at this time of year – but do buy them early in order to get what you want, rather than at the last moment. I've been known to buy Christmas decorations in the middle of a hot summer from one of those wonderful Christmas decoration shops all over the United States.

Although you can go to town on decorating the house in general, create the main party theme in the middle of the tea table as I've done in the picture on page 138. The basic idea was of a large bursting Christmas cracker – here about 75 cm (30 inches) long – which I made from rolled thin cardboard covered with crêpe paper and studded with stars. Into the middle of the cracker I very carefully cut a hole, not a large round one, but various lengths of cuts radiating out from a central incision. It looked like an exploding star, and its main benefit was that it would help keep the central arrangement steady. Into the opening, I then wedged a large piece of styrofoam weighted with plasticine for additional ballast. Thereafter the arrangement was made as with fresh material but, as you can see, it's anything but! It took a long time to collect all these bits and pieces, and they come from many parts of the world – but above all they are colourful. All 'ingredients' without stems had stems added: a wooden skewer was pushed into each small Christmas cracker, and were taped to the sticks of rock and candy. The main thing to remember about an arrangement such as this, apart from colour (and as much sugary edibility as possible), is to ensure that there is a gift in it for every child at the party.

This cracker idea could easily be adapted for *any* party, and not just for children. One Christmas I designed a setting in black and gold with a central large black cracker, decorated with the gold foil trimming sold by the yard to go round cakes. Instead of edible goodies, I had a bursting gold arrangement with lots of sparkle. At each place setting I had black place mats – cardboard covered with plain black paper and a decorative edge similar to that on the golden wedding place mats. Individual black and gold crackers were placed alongside and it ended up one of the classiest table settings I have ever created. Once again, you see, when the old mind gets working, you never know what wondrous inventions you might come up with!

CHRISTMAS

Christmas is a fantastic time for the flower arranger, and it is very definitely my favourite time of year – as anyone who knows me, who has seen my demonstrations or has read my previous books will know. The house can be decorated in so many different ways and in so many different places, only a few of which I can cover here.

MATERIALS FOR CHRISTMAS ARRANGEMENTS

The first thing to consider – whether you are decorating your own home or have been asked to decorate someone else's – is the *kind* of Christmas it is to be, traditional or not. To me, it's *always* traditional, with Christmas plant materials – holly, ivy and a tree – and the archetypal Christmas colours of reds, golds and silvers.

The next thing to think about is the durability of your chosen materials: you want them to last over the festive season, on to Twelfth Night if possible. Thus I tend to think in terms of artificial materials at Christmas, which nowadays are so splendid, there cannot possibly be any shame in using them. In centrally heated homes, they are a godsend, and once finished with for one season, they can be stored for the next.

RINGS AND GARLANDS

One of the first festive and welcoming ideas could be a welcome ring on the front door: I describe how to start one

In a basically black and white hall, I decorated the white staircase with an artificial green garland, held at the top of the sweeps with large red satin ribbon bows. The colourful decorations on the garland are what are known as 'fruit picks' in the trade – commercial clusters of artificial fruit and leaves, all with their own wire stems. These fix in easily wherever you want in the garland. They come in so many different colourings and groupings, their only disadvantage is that you're spoiled for choice! Festooning a staircase thus leaves the table free to display the collection of hatpins under a Victorian glass dome.

on page 121, and I'm sure, with the wealth of Christmas materials available, an idea will immediately spring to mind of how to adapt it for Christmas. The next Christmas arrangement might be in the hall. At this time, with all its decorative possibilities, you may wish to put away some of the bits and pieces usually on display. In the photograph on page 143, however, I wished to retain the Victorian glass dome – filled with some of my wife Pat's collection of Whitby jet and pearl hatpins – so I decorated the staircase instead of the table top. This is an idea you may have seen before but, as you see, the red of the ribbon and the green of the (artificial) garland really cheer up the largely white hall. I can't emphasize enough how useful I consider these garlands: I've had some now for 20 years and I'm still ringing the changes on what I can do with them. The garlands here were wired, so I could make them into any shape I wanted. One point to note is that I always advise fixing the garland into place *before* attaching the decorative objects: that way you can ensure that all of the decorations are at the front, where you want them to be, rather than spinning around the back where they'd be wasted. I still had some ribbon left after making the red bows at the top of the sweeps of the garland – so made one to match for the lamp. Very festive!

HANGING ARRANGEMENTS

Another idea which can be used when you don't want to put away too many of your personal things – it's your *home*, after all – is the hanging arrangement. I've used this before when there wasn't much space available for arrangements, but at

Christmas it can look wonderful, filling up a corner without taking any valuable table space. The inspiration for this particular arrangement was the red Spanish wall rug and the red macramé plant-pot hanger. The colour, of course, was echoed by ribbon bows and flowers – and it may surprise you that I used poinsettia – *the* Christmas flowering pot plant – as a cut flower in the arrangement. They do stand up well to this sort of treatment, but you must condition them properly first. When cut, the stems exude a milky sap, so you must seal the ends (see page 11). Thereafter I stand them in cold water for about 12 hours before arranging.

TREES

Trees of all shapes have always been of great interest to me and the Christmas tree most of all – the introduction of which was due to Prince Albert. Although I've written and spoken so much over the years about Christmas trees, there is still so much to say. I think, though, that the Americans have got it right, treating the tree as yet another flower arrangement, with a definite colour scheme. What about, you might ask, all those trimmings you've been collecting and storing for the last 20 years? Well, just start again, is my answer, if you want to create a really unified look. The trees are basically green and there's so much interesting that can be done with that green as a background: all red bows, all gold or silver baubles, all little colourful parcels.

In the picture on page 147, however, I have *created* a tree shape rather than use a real tree (the same idea as in church, see page 54). The stand itself was a very simple wood

Above: A hanging arrangement looks wonderful at any time, but at Christmas, when space is short, it can be the answer to a number of problems. Against the background of a red Spanish wall rug, I hung a red string macramé holder and inserted a round-bottomed bowl filled with soaked floral foam. Traditional Christmas foliages – as ever – were the first placements: pine, cypress, holly and ivy spray out from all sides. A large red ribbon bow was inserted and then the flowers, red carnations and poinsettias, which were conditioned very well in advance so that they would last.

Right: This small Christmas tree may look real, but in fact it's 'home-made', achieved by working in tandem three containers attached to a strong spine batten. The principal foliage is natural treated yew, sprayed with artificial snow. Delicate plastic sprays with some glitter added a different outline, together with some large snowflake shapes which were given wire stems. Once the basic pyramid was formed, I added textural interest with white velvet ribbon bows, a lovely combination with the snow-covered branches. The bauble collection – all on wooden skewers (see page 129) – added texture as well, some being traditional glass, while others are covered in lurex.

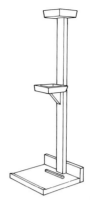

The home-made wooden stand on which was created the green and white tree. (The same idea was used in the wall arrangement in church, see page 54.) Any number of levels could be created, rather than just the three here.

construction. A base of about 30 × 25 cm (12 × 10 inches) had a 1.2 m (4 ft) batten screwed to one long side as a spine: at this stage it looked rather like a long-handled shovel. To this spine a small bracket was fixed half-way up, and to this was screwed a container. Another container was screwed to a bracket on the top, and another container rested on the base. Thus I had three levels to work with. Blocks of styrofoam were wedged into each of the three areas, and the three areas – very important this – were then worked together so that a general tapering shape was made. The outline material was one of the most interesting I've worked with for years – natural yew, treated (but don't ask me how), and then most of it sprayed with artificial snow. Done well, this spraying looks very good, but it must be generously applied – a blob here and there gives the impression a bird has just flown over! When the three sections together had combined to make the pyramid shape, I added ribbon bows and baubles. The colour scheme was obviously green, silver and white, but you could use whatever you like or whatever would suit your home. This is just the basic idea, and as long as you stick to one colour scheme it will work. (As an alternative, think about the possibilities of a lovely shaped bare branch. Either left in its near black state or sprayed a colour – white or silver, say – it could look magnificent if decorated with the right accessories and placed in the right setting.)

FRUIT

I like using fruit in arrangements at this festive time of year and it always surprises me when people say 'How nice, why didn't I think of that?' To me fruit is just as 'arrangeable' as are flowers – and, after all, Mother Nature produced them both. Go along to your local fruit and vegetable shop and look at the colours, shapes and sizes – aren't they interesting? And you don't have to buy the shop either; in most cases one or two examples of each shape is all that is needed. It's the variety of sizes, though, that I think most important. In a flower arrangement, you cannot do a good job with flowers all one size, and it's the same with fruit.

Christmas and mounds of fruit seem to go together – whether because of the over-buying we all seem to be guilty of then, or so that we can counteract all that over-indulgence, I don't know. Traditionally those mounds of fruit are simply placed into a large bowl, once Grannie's, which appears from the back of the cupboard where it has languished all the rest of the year. How uninteresting, I say, because so much more can be done with it. By all means have a bowl of fruit for the between- or mid-meal raiders, but try to create something a little more adventurous with some of it. Incorporate some foliage, which will break up all those round shapes. Hide a small container of soaked floral foam in the bottom of the bowl, into which you can poke pieces of foliage; this makes all the difference to the look of the finished group. The fruit in the middle of the silver epergne on page 150 is quite considerably enhanced by the addition of some foliage, don't you think? (Incidentally, when mounting fruit, always use wooden skewers or wooden cocktail sticks – which simply make a little hole in the fruit – rather than florist's stub wire. If you use the latter, rust sets in very quickly and the fruit cannot be eaten after the arrangement is dismantled.)

With the sparkling glasses, and napkins held together with gold strings and topped with crackers, my red and green Christmas table looks very festive. In the central dish of the epergne I arranged wooden-skewer-stemmed fruit with pieces of holly and ivy and a couple of bows pushed in between to soften all the round shapes. The dishes at the two sides of the epergne were worked together with western hemlock as outline foliage, along with holly and variegated ivy. Red ribbon bows were then inserted to link in with the bows among the fruit, before the flowers — red spray carnations and red 'Mercedes' roses — were divided into two lots and arranged. It's a good, generous, colourful and welcoming setting.

A napkin ring idea used at the green and white wedding earlier in the book. The artificial flowers and foliages and the ribbons complement the wedding flower and colour scheme in general, as well as the streamers radiating out from the table-centre arrangement (see page 95).

And what Christmas party would be complete without a grand lunch or dinner. This is where you can really go over the top and make the table setting very special. I'm a sentimental traditionalist, so I've made my table on page 150 basic Christmas greens and reds, using flowers, fruit, foliage, silver and glass. It all looks very festive though, with the red cloth, green Wedgwood plates, a pair of German silver and ivory drinking horns (used often as containers, not just as accessories) and one of my more prized possessions, a silver Victorian epergne. It is divided into three sections, each holding a glass dish. It's a gem of a container, and was used by the Victorians as a table centrepiece to hold fruit – so my usage, flowers *plus* fruit, would have earned their approval.

NAPKIN RINGS

I've mentioned home-made napkin rings so often already, it's perhaps inappropriate to bring them in at the end of the book, but they're so decorative and cheerful in the massed picture on page 154 that they look Christmassy!

Many of you will be expert at making those elaborate shapes out of damask napkins, and will think, why bother with making napkin rings. However, I'm not too keen on the shapes because they can over-clutter a table, and don't forget, as a flower arranger, it's flowers and creativity that come first with me when it comes to decor.

They are very simple to make. The bases are the centre cardboard tube of a toilet paper roll. One tube carefully cut can make three rings, but you must use a good sharp knife or razor blade. Choose your colour scheme, get together your chosen bits and pieces and your glue, and get cracking!

The wedding napkin ring on page 151 was covered with a white ribbon overlaid with a white lace ribbon, making sure the joins were in the same place. I gathered the small group of silk flowers and leaves in my fingers into a bunch and wired them together with florist's reel wire, then I fixed the bow. The whole group was then glued on to the ring, over the ribbon joins, in one go. I added a simple place card, a must for large parties, but they can be more elaborate.

The two rings at the bottom of the picture on page 154 are as elaborate looking but just as simple to make. In each case the backing is ribbon, but you could of course use wrapping paper or even wallpaper cut into strips. If there is going to be a lot of decoration, though, try to keep the backing as plain as possible, and always finish off the edges with some sort of braiding to add interest (and to cover the cut ends). The pink flowers ring could be for a girl's coming of age party or a wedding anniversary party with a pink colour scheme; the silver and pearl collection could be an idea for a silver wedding celebration. The green and red one at top right is very Christmassy with its hint of gold – and the one in the centre is simply a red ring, trimmed around the middle rather than the edges, topped with a stick-on parcel bow. The drum ring could be ideal for a children's party. The red ribbon is decorated with leftover strips of metallic lampshade braid, glued to the edge along with some narrow gold ribbon. The drumsticks are two wooden cocktail sticks with an old bead glued to one end and sprayed gold. All very simple, and I hope I've fired your imaginations – indeed I hope I've done that throughout the entire book.

A selection of colourful and entertaining home-made napkin rings, designed to suit any sort of celebration. Not only do they add to a colour scheme, making a table look more interesting, they could also be taken home afterwards as a memento of the occasion.

PLANT GLOSSARY

Alchemilla (*mollis*, lady's mantle)
Allium (*cepa*/onion, *sativum*/garlic)
Alstroemeria (Peruvian lily)
Ananas (pineapple plant)
Anemone (windflower)
Anthriscus sylvestris (cow parsley, Queen Anne's lace)
Apple (*malus sylvestris*)
Artichoke (*cynara scolymus*)
Asparagus fern (*asparagus plumosus*)

Baby's breath (*gysophila paniculata*, Bristol fairy)
Bean pod
Beech (*fagus*)
Bellis perennis (daisy)
Bells of Ireland (*molucella laevis*)
Bergenia (*saxifraga*, elephant's ears)
Betula pendula (silver birch)
Bouvardia (*longiflora*)
Box (*buxus*)
Bristol fairy (*gypsophila paniculata*, baby's breath)
Broom (*cytisus, genista*)
Butcher's broom (*ruscus aculeatus*)
Buxus (box)

Cactus, dried
Cape gooseberry (*physalis*)
Carnation (*dianthus caryophyllus*, single/spray)
Centaurea cyanus (cornflower)
Chinese lantern (*physalis*)
Chlorophytum elatum (spider plant)
Christmas rose (*helleborus niger*)
Chrysanthemum (anemone-flowered, *frutescans*/marguerite, pompon, single/double flowered, spider, spray)
Citrus sinensis (orange)
Conium maculatum (hemlock)
Convallaria majalis (lily of the valley)
Cornflower (*centaurea cyanus*)
Cotoneaster
Cow parsley (*anthriscus sylvestris*)
Cucurbita pepo (ornamental gourd)
Cupressus (true cypress)
Cymbidium (orchid)
Cypress, true (*cupressus*)
Cytisus (broom)

Daffodil (*narcissus*)
Dahlia
Daisy (*Bellis perennis*)
Dendrobium (orchid)
Dianthus caryophyllus (pink, carnation, 'Crowley's Sim', 'White Sim', 'William Sim', 'Yellow Dusty Sim')

Erica (heath, heather)
Eucalyptus (gum tree)
Euphorbia (*griffithii, palustris, polychroma, pulcherrima*/poinsettia, *robiae, wulfenii*)

Fagus (beech, *cuprea*/copper, *sylvatica*/common)
Ferns (asparagus/*asparagus plumosus*, hart's-tongue/*phyllitis scolopendrium*, ladder/*nephrolepis*, leather, royal/*osmunda regalis*)
Flax, New Zealand (*phormium tenax*)
Freesia

Garlic (*allium sativum*)
Genista (broom)
Gerbera (Transvaal daisy)
Giant hogweed (*heracleum mantegazzianum*)
Gladiolus (gladioli, sword lily)
Gourd, ornamental (*cucubita pepo*)
Grape (*vitis*)
Gum tree (*eucalyptus*)
Gypsophila (*paniculata*, Bristol fairy, baby's breath)

Hawthorn (*crataegus monogyna*, may)
Heath, heather (*erica*)
Hedera (ivy, *canariensis*/Canary Island, *helix*/common, 'Buttercup', 'Glacier', 'Goldheart', 'Sulphur Heart')
Helleborus (*niger*, Christmas rose)
Hemlock (*conium maculatum*)
Heracleum mantegazzianum (giant hogweed)
Holly (*ilex*)
Hosta (plantain lily, *albomarginata, crispula, fortunei*/'Albopicta', *sieboldiana, undulata*, etc)
Hyacinth (*hyacinthus, orientalis albulus*/Roman hyacinth)

Hydrangea

Ilex (holly)
Iris
Ivy (*hedera*)

Ladder fern (*nephrolepis*)
Lady's mantle (*alchemilla mollis*)
Laurel (*laurus*)
Leather fern
Leucospermum cordifolium (pincushion protea)
Lilac (*syringa*)
Lily (*lilium*, 'Connecticut King', 'Enchantment', *longiflorum*, 'Mont Blanc', Peruvian/*alstroemeria*, plantain/hosta)
Lily of the valley (*convallaria majalis*)
Limonium (sea lavender, sea statice)

Mahogany pod
Malus sylvestris (apple)
Maranta leuconeura (prayer plant)
Marguerite (*chrysanthemum frutescans*)
May (*crataegus monogyna*), hawthorn
Michaelmas daisy (*aster*, mini-mic)
Mini-mic (Michaelmas daisy, *aster*)
Molucella laevis (bells of Ireland)

Narcissus (daffodil)
Nephrolepis fern (ladder fern)
New Zealand flax (*phormium tenax*)

Onion (*allium cepa*)
Orange (*citrus sinensis*)
Orchid (*cymbidium*, *dendrobium*/Singapore orchid)
Osmunda regalis (royal fern)

Papaver (poppy)
Periwinkle (*vinca*)
Peruvian lily (*alstroemeria*)
Philadelphus (mock orange)
Phormium tenax (New Zealand flax)
Phyllitis scolopendrium (hart's-tongue fern)

Physalis (Cape gooseberry, Chinese lantern)
Pineapple plant (*ananas*)
Pine (*pinus*)
Pine cones
Pink (*dianthus*)
Pinus (pine)
Plantain lily (hosta)
Poinsettia (*euphorbia pulcherrima*)
Pomegranate (*punica granatum*)
Poppy (*papaver*)
Prayer plant *(maranta leuconeura)*
Protea (pincushion, *leucospermum cordifolium*)
Prunus (plum, ornamental cherry)
Punica granatum (pomegranate)

Queen Anne's lace (*anthriscus sylvestris*)

Rose (*rosa*, 'Bridal Pink', 'Carina', 'Champagne', 'Golden Times', 'Mercedes', 'Sonia', 'Tiara', etc)
Ruscus (*aculeatus*, butcher's broom)

Saxifraga (bergenia, elephant's ears)
Sea grape leaves
Sea statice (*limonium*)
Silver birch (*betula pendula*)
Singapore orchid (*dendrobium*)
Spider plant (*chlorophytum elatum*)
Stephanotis (*floribunda*)
Stock (*malcolmia*)
Sword lily (*gladiolus*)
Syringa (lilac)

Taxus (yew)
Tsuga heterophylla (western hemlock)
Tulip (*tulipa*)

Vinca (periwinkle)
Violet (*viola*)

Weigela (*florida*)
Western hemlock (*tsuga heterophylla*)
Windflower (anemone)

INDEX

Accessories, 13, 93, 116, 118, 119, 126, 127, 152
Advance planning, 8, 33–7, 89–90
Alabaster, 15, 107, 109
Alstroemeria, 27, 107
All-round arrangements, 93–7, 100–104, 107, 109–10, 113–20, 124–5, 127–8, 130, 132–41
Altar arrangements, 35, 38, 39, 41–4, 67
Altar vases, 44, 117
Anemones, 10, 78
Anniversary, *see* Wedding anniversary
Apples, 43, 46, 51, 52, 114, 123
Artichoke bottoms, dried, 24
Artificial plant materials, 21, 24, 51–3, 55–6, 72, 78, 82–5, 97, 98, 99, 101, 128, 129, 131, 143, 151
Artificial snow, 146–8

Baby's breath, *see* Bristol fairy
Ball tree, 103, 105, 140
Bases, 114, 119
    to make, 117, 120
Baskets/basketry, 7, 15, 25–6, 121
    arrangements, 7, 25–6, 29, 30, 43, 45, 46, 47, 55, 56, 92, 106, 108, 109, 110–11
    bridesmaid's, 45, 71, 72–3, 83, 85
Bathroom, 16, 29–32
Baubles, 125, 126, 127, 128, 131, 146–8
    stems for, 129, 132, 145
Bean pods, dried, 30, 119
Bedroom, 17, 26–9
Bedsits, 29, 113, 118
Beech, 18, 38, 40
Bells of Ireland, 58
Bergenia, 18
Berries, 53, 74, 75, 79, 86, 120, 126
Bouquets, 34, 68, 69–81, 84, 85, 88, 110
Bouvardia, 103, 134
Bows, *see* Ribbon
Box, 38, 53, 54, 103, 105, 120
Braiding, 117, 153
Bridal flowers, 8, 34, 68–88
    bouquets, 34, 68, 69–81, 84, 85, 88, 110
    bridesmaid's basket, 45, 71, 72–3, 83, 85
    buttonholes, 85, 88

    corsages, 85, 88
    handbag spray, 88
    headdresses, 75, 78–86, 88
Bristol fairy (baby's breath), 27, 38, 39, 41, 46, 49, 54, 55, 58, 63, 66, 70, 71, 78, 79, 81, 102, 103, 105, 106, 107, 110, 111, 118, 127, 138, 139
Broom, 7, 66, 67, 107
Buffet parties, 6, 17, 93, 112, 132–3, 134
Buttonholes, 85, 88
Buying flowers, 9–10

Cactus, dried, 119
Cake boards, 120, 125, 128, 130
Cake table, 98, 99, 100–104
Candles, 44, 90, 91, 96, 113, 114, 115, 125, 126, 130, 134
Candle-cup holders, 14, 20, 96
Candle galleries, 125, 130
Candlesticks, 14, 44, 125, 130, 131
Cape gooseberries, 24
Carnations, 7, 18, 30, 38, 39, 41, 53, 55, 58, 59, 62, 66, 88, 102, 103, 106, 107, 123, 134, 135, 138, 139, 146
    spray, 40, 43, 46, 49, 54, 59, 62, 63, 67, 71, 78, 90, 91, 103, 110, 111, 114, 123, 134, 138, 139, 151
Cathedral, 33, 34, 57, 59
Champagne, 110–11, 128
Chancel and screen, 35, 38–41
Chapel, 6, 33, 64, 65, 66, 67
Children's parties, 6, 112, 120, 136–41, 153
China, 113, 115, 128, 152
Christenings, 61, 64, 137
Christmas, 6, 8, 21, 53, 75, 77, 80, 85, 86, 120, 128, 129, 138, 140–41, 142–53
    crackers, 138, 140–41
    hanging arrangements, 144–5
    materials, 142, 148–9
    rings and garlands, 142–4
    table setting, 150, 152
    trees, 142, 145–8
    weddings, 75, 77, 80, 85
Christmas rose, 75, 86
Chrysanthemum, 18, 38, 41
    bloom, 57, 58
    pompon, 46, 49
    spray, 18, 30, 40, 59, 62, 63, 67, 74, 90,

Chrysanthemum (cont.)
91, 103, 106, 107, 114, 115, 118,
123, 130, 134
Church, 6, 7, 21, 33–67
Cocktail sticks, 96, 149, 153
Coming of age parties, 112, 132–6, 153
Conditioning, 9, 10–12, 26, 37, 76, 145,
146
Containers, 9, 14–15, 18, 19, 20, 36, 100,
101, 115, 116, 118, 124, 127, 129, 133,
135, 136, 137, 148, 149, 152
Corn, 126
Cornflower, 78
Coronet, *see* Headdresses
Corsages, 85, 88
Cotoneaster, 74
Cow parsley, 69, 72
Crackers, 138, 140–41, 151
Cutlery, 113, 115, 128
Cypress, 52, 146

Daffodil, 66, 67, 112
Dahlia, 59
Daisy, 27
Dinner parties, 6, 16, 17, 112, 113, 118,
152
'Doves', 93, 99, 101, 119
Dried materials, 21–5, 30, 78, 79,
116–17, 119, 135

Entrance arrangements, 17–20, 53–7,
104–5, 120, 128–9, 131, 142–4
Equipment, 12–14
Eucalyptus, 123
Euphorbia, 11

Fern, 17, 27, 38, 43, 53, 54, 55, 88
artificial, 128, 129, 131
asparagus, 78
dried, 24, 123
leather, 30, 46
nephrolepis, 18, 114, 115, 130
when to pick, 48
Floral foam, 7, 13, 20, 24, 29, 30, 36, 39,
41, 44, 48, 55, 56, 60, 64, 71, 96, 97,
103, 105, 108, 114, 117, 118, 123, 124,
134, 138, 146, 149
Floral foam tape, 13, 20, 57, 61, 96, 132
Florist's flowers, 9, 10, 36, 37, 112
Florist's stem tape, 13, 22, 24, 101
Florist's wires, 13, 21–2, 24, 28, 65,
76–7, 84, 88, 97, 101, 133, 149, 153

Flower cones and tubes, 13, 56, 57, 58,
60
Flower festivals, 37, 61
Foliages, 27, 40, 46, 49, 52, 53, 90, 96,
138, 139, 146, 149, 150, 152
conditioning, 10–12, 37, 126
Fonts, 60–64, 69–70
Freesia, 67, 71, 74, 90, 91, 114, 115, 130
Freeze-dried materials, 81
Fruit, 43, 46, 48, 51, 52, 90, 114, 117,
123, 126, 148–52
artificial, 51, 119, 123, 125, 126, 127,
128, 143
mirror, 125, 127
stems for, 149
'picks', 143

Garden cane, 14, 22, 24, 56, 57, 58, 60,
65, 110, 138, 139
Garlands, 21, 29, 49–53, 94
artificial, 21, 50–53, 55, 56, 93, 102,
126, 143
in church, 52–6
dried (swag), 21–4, 76
fresh, 21, 49–52
as headdresses, 84–5
in marquees, 105, 108
on staircases, 21–4, 109, 143, 144
on tables, 94, 98, 99, 100, 101
Garlic, 126
Gerbera, 7, 18, 26, 59, 62, 107, 110, 111,
135
conditioning, 26
Giant hogweed, 135
Gladioli, 38, 39, 40, 58, 59, 60
Glass, 15, 30–32, 51, 120, 124, 125, 127,
146–8
Glue, 14, 117, 153
Golden wedding anniversary, 124,
125–32, 141
Gourds, 117, 119, 123
Grapes, 43, 51, 52, 90, 91, 96, 97, 114,
119, 123, 125
Grape vine cuttings, 116, 123

Half-band, *see* Headdresses
Hall, 17–20, 55, 128, 144
Handbag spray, 88
Hanging arrangements, 20, 55, 56, 92–3,
108, 109, 144–5, 146
Harvest festival, 46, 120
Hawthorn, 69

Headdresses, 75, 78–85, 86–7
  bride's, 78, 81–5, 87
  bridesmaid's, 75, 78–85, 86
  measuring, 84
Heath, heather, 62, 63, 78, 134
Hellebores, 11, 75
Hemlock, 69
Holly, 75, 86, 120, 142, 146, 151
Hosta, 38, 39, 40, 43, 46
Hyacinth, 64–5, 66
Hydrangea, 11

Ikebana, 12, 13
Iris, 7, 38, 43, 67, 102
Ivy, 17, 18, 38, 39, 46, 51, 55, 59, 60, 69,
  70, 71, 74, 75, 77, 78, 82, 86, 90, 91,
  114, 118, 123, 134, 142, 146, 151

Lady's mantle, 38, 41, 43, 46, 49, 54, 55,
  90, 91
Landing, 7, 25–6
Laurel, 58
Lilac, 11, 69
Lily, 18, 69, 74, 78, 102, 123
  longiflorum, 38, 39, 41, 107
  Peruvian, 27, 107
Lily of the valley, 70, 74, 104
'Line' arrangements, 13, 15
Linen flowers, 71, 72, 97
Lurex materials, 124, 127, 129, 130,
  146–8

Mahogany pods, 119
Marguerites, 38, 53, 54, 55
Marquee, 34, 89, 90, 102, 103, 104–6,
  108
May blossom, 69
Mechanics, 9, 12–14, 36, 40, 60, 90, 91
Michaelmas daisy, 38
Mini-mic, 38, 41, 46, 49, 55
Mirrors, 129, 131, 132

Napkins, 113, 114, 115, 128, 136, 151,
  152
Napkin rings, 95, 97, 128, 151, 154
  to make, 152–3
New Zealand flax, 18

Onion, 126
Orange, 123
Orange blossom, 80
Orchid, 18, 107

Singapore, 62, 70, 74, 77, 90, 91, 110,
  111, 127
  'stems' for, 109–10
Parasols, paper, 137, 138, 139
Parties, 16, 89–111, 112–41, 142–53
Pearl sprays, 70, 82, 104
Pedestal arrangements, 35, 40–41, 59,
  60, 92
Periwinkle, 71
Pew-end arrangements, 35, 46, 48–9, 63,
  64, 133, 134
Philadelphus, 11
Pine, 52, 146
Pineapple, 123
Pine cones, 21, 24, 126
  stems for, 21–2
Pinholders, 13, 119
Pinks, 27, 30
Place cards, 90, 151
Place mats, 125, 128, 130, 135, 136, 141
Plasticine, 13, 14, 20, 140
Poinsettia, 145, 146
Polyester materials, 84
Pomegranates, 117, 119
Poppy, 11
  dried heads, 24, 123
Porch, 17–18, 27
Posy, see Bouquets
Prayer plant, 18
Presents, 29, 30, 73, 110–11, 141, 152,
  154
  hanging, 137, 140
Preserved materials, 18, 21–5, 116–17
Protea, pincushion, 30
Prunus, 63
Pulpits, 60–62
Pyramid arrangements, 21–5, 56–8

Reception, see Wedding reception
Registry office, 65, 67
Ribbon, 72, 95, 97, 108, 123, 152
  bows, 27, 28–9, 46, 49, 51, 52, 53, 55,
    56, 63, 64, 71, 73, 79, 83, 100, 101, 102,
    105, 106, 110, 111, 126, 133, 134,
    137, 138, 139, 143, 144, 145, 146,
    151, 153
  bows, to make, 28–9
  to curl, 105–6
  streamers, 28, 55, 75, 78, 79, 83, 85, 86,
    95, 97, 100, 103, 105, 134, 138, 139,
    151

Ring, *see* Welcome ring
Rose, 10, 20, 63, 70, 71, 74, 78, 79, 80, 82, 88, 90, 91, 102, 104, 105, 107, 112, 115, 118, 127, 130, 151
  Christmas, 75
  leaves, 78, 79, 90, 91, 115
Ruscus, 59, 60, 64, 66, 102, 106, 107, 123, 134

Scissors, 12
Sea grape leaves, 116, 119
Sea statice, dried, 55, 56
Secateurs, 12
Seed pods, 21, 24, 79
  stems for, 21–2
Silk materials, 21–5, 70, 71, 72, 82, 84, 97, 123, 129, 131, 138, 139, 153
Silver birch, 93
Silver wedding anniversary, 124–5, 127, 153
Sitting room, 22, 107, 109, 128
Skewers, wooden, 129, 132, 145, 149, 151
Spelter, 20, 25
Spider plant, 38, 51, 52, 123
St Mary's, Luddenden, 38
Staircase, 20–25, 55–6, 109, 143, 144
Stand, wooden, 53, 54, 145, 147, 148
Stems, 10–12, 21–2, 109–10
  fresh, 10–12
  taping, 22, 76
  wire, 21–2, 30, 73, 76, 123, 143
  wooden, 129, 132, 145, 149, 151
Stephanotis, 70, 74, 82
Styrofoam (dry foam), 13, 24, 101, 119, 123, 129, 132, 140, 148
Swag, *see* Garland
Synagogue, 6, 33, 49

Table arrangements, 89, 90, 91, 93–103, 112, 113–16, 129, 130, 131, 137–41, 150–52
Tablecloth, 113, 128, 136, 138, 152
Table streamers, 95, 97, 151
Table swags, 98, 99, 100–101, 133

Thanksgiving parties, 120–24, 137
Top table, 97–100
'Tree' arrangements, 54, 103, 105, 140, 142, 145–8
Tulip, 11, 63, 66
Twelfth Night, 142
Twin arrangements, 40–41

Vegetables, 48, 126, 149
  stems for, 149
Violet, 11

Watering can, 14
Wedding, 6, 14, 21, 33–67, 133, 151, 153
  budget, 33–4, 57, 90, 93, 106
  church flowers, 33–67
  colour scheme, 33, 34, 38, 85, 90, 94, 151
Wedding anniversary parties, 6, 111, 124–32, 153
Wedding cake, 89, 97, 98, 99, 104
  decoration, 98, 99, 101
  table, 98, 99, 100–104
Wedding reception, 8, 21, 34, 89–111
  colour scheme, 89, 109, 151
  flowers for, 90–97, 104–8, 113
  in marquee, 102–3, 104–8
  tables for, 93–4, 100–108
Weigela, 11
Welcome arrangements, 16–32, 90–93, 102–6, 109, 112, 121–4
Welcome ring, 17, 120–21, 123, 126, 131, 132, 142–4
Western hemlock, 7, 39, 62, 64, 66, 102, 106, 107, 151
Wheat, dried, 24, 123
Wickerwork, 15, 121, 126, 137, 138, 139
Window-sill arrangements, 43, 44–8, 64–5
Wire cutters, 12
Wire netting (mesh), 13, 24, 36, 56, 60
Wood roses, 116, 119

Yew, 146–8